THE SOCIAL PROBLEM IN THE
PHILOSOPHY OF ROUSSEAU

Cambridge Studies in the History and Theory of Politics

EDITORS

MAURICE COWLING
G. R. ELTON
E. KEDOURIE
J. G. A. POCOCK
J. R. POLE
WALTER ULLMANN

For complete list of books in this series see page 147

THE SOCIAL PROBLEM
IN THE
PHILOSOPHY OF ROUSSEAU

JOHN CHARVET

Lecturer in Government,
London School of Economics

CAMBRIDGE UNIVERSITY PRESS

CAMBRIDGE

LONDON · NEW YORK · MELBOURNE

Published by the Syndics of the Cambridge University Press
The Pitt Building, Trumpington Street, Cambridge CB2 1RP
Bentley House, 200 Euston Road, London NW1 2DB
32 East 57th Street, New York, NY 10022, USA
296 Beaconsfield Parade, Middle Park, Melbourne 3206, Australia

Library of Congress catalogue card number: 73–88311

ISBN 0 521 20189 6

First published 1974
Reprinted 1978

Printed in Great Britain
at the Alden Press, Oxford
Reprinted in Great Britain at the
University Press, Cambridge

CONTENTS

CONTENTS

ACKNOWLEDGEMENTS

I am very grateful to Shirley Letwin and Christopher Cherry for their detailed comments on the content of earlier versions of this essay, and again to Shirley Letwin and my sister, Anne Charvet, for their attempts to improve its style.

John Charvet

August 1973

I

INTRODUCTION

In this book I provide a critical reconstruction of the major steps in the argument of three of Rousseau's works: the *Discourse on the Origins of Inequality*, *Emile* and the *Social Contract*. My interest in doing this lies with the problem that Rousseau presents and develops in these works about the individual's relations to others in society. My reason for selecting only these three from the body of Rousseau's writing is that they are the major statements of his mature thought on the subject and that taken together they constitute a unified argument. By concentrating on them I can isolate and criticize the essential steps in Rousseau's reasoning about the individual in his social relations. As the first part of his argument the *Discourse on the Origins of Inequality* (first published in 1755) contains an account of how the social conditions of men's existence create for them a fundamental problem as to their individual identities. It is the preliminary presentation and analysis of the social problem. *Emile* (first published in 1762) and the *Social Contract* (first published also in 1762) are attempts to conceive the solution to it. *Emile* provides an account of the educational and moral relations, and the *Social Contract* the political relations that must be realized between men for the problem to be solved.

The initial concern which gave rise to Rousseau's enterprise can be expressed in terms of his well-known belief that man is by nature good and only corrupted in society. To show that this is so is what he undertakes in the *Discourse on the Origins of Inequality*, to reveal uncorrupted human nature on the one hand, and corrupted social man on the other. The definition of both the goodness and the corruption of human nature presents Rousseau with the problem which his subsequent work attempts to solve: how to conceive of a society and social relations between men in which this corruption is avoided and the potentialities in human nature for virtue are fully developed. The terms in which the goodness and corruption, and so the social problem are defined by Rousseau thus constitute the centre around

I

which his intellectual enterprise is constructed and through which, if the terms are fundamentally misconceived, it must fail.

The essence of the corruption involves a certain sort of relationship of the individual to others. While this corrupt relationship has its necessary material conditions, namely economic interdependence, it is constituted not by economic relations, but by the sort of consciousness the individual has of himself in his relations to others. It is a consciousness of his individuality in which he comes to have for himself the identity and value that he has in the eyes of others. The individual becomes for himself what Rousseau holds to be an artificial creation out of the opinions of others. This essentially other-dependent consciousness makes it necessary for men to please others in order to be satisfied with themselves. As a result they lose their natural liberty to determine for themselves their own identity and value, and instead have these imposed on them by others.

The root of the social problem for Rousseau is this other-dependent consciousness, which Rousseau claims is not integral to human nature but only the artificial product of society. What Rousseau attempts to do is to reconcile nature and society by conceiving of a way in which men may be related to each other in society which nevertheless excludes this freedom-destroying and corrupting dependence. What is required is the development of a new consciousness, which will enable men to conceive of themselves in their relation with others in such a way that no one is dependent but all remain unrestricted and free.

The way in which Rousseau initially defines the problem of dependence is in terms of a contrast between nature and society where the idea of nature is represented by the concept of a state of nature, a condition of man in which no society exists and no social relations are experienced. This non-social nature is characterized as good and contrasted to society as corrupt, for in nature there is no dependence of men on each other, but only in society. However, Rousseau proposes to resolve the problem of dependence in society by returning to nature in the sense of refounding society on nature, and this project creates a paradox which lies at the centre of Rousseau's ultimate incoherence. For there is no dependence in nature because there are no social relations. In the formation of society the independence of nature must necessarily be destroyed, and yet if society is to be made tolerable for men it must recreate the independence of nature. The good society, for Rousseau, must both denature man and yet be founded upon man's nature. In my critical reconstruction of Rousseau's argument I shall show why this paradox arises and how its dissolution involves the dissolution of Rousseau's whole enterprise.

This book is not a commentary on Rousseau's social and political thought in general. It is not even a full commentary on the three works I am considering. Much in these works that is peripheral to the crucial steps in the development of the argument will be ignored. For what I hope to achieve in concentrating on these crucial steps is to get to the root of Rousseau's conception of the social problem, to reveal the fundamental presuppositions which govern both the terms in which he presents the problem and the terms in which the solution to it is conceived. In doing so I aim to show that because of these presuppositions his social problem is misconceived and his solution radically incoherent.

The critical nature of this enterprise supposes that Rousseau's problems and ideas are of interest to us in other ways than as a mere episode in the history of past thought, an episode that may have historical significance but is without current philosophical relevance. Of course, subsequent thought has moved on from Rousseau, and does not confront its problems in exactly the same terms as Rousseau uses. Nevertheless it is the assumption of this work that the problems Rousseau raises about the nature of the individual's relations to others in society have remained in different guises the unresolved concern of later thinkers. I do not deliberately attempt to show that this is so, but assume it and leave it to the reader, should he find any interest in my argument, to reflect on it in the light of this assumption.

It must be stressed that this work is not a history of Rousseau's thought. It does not present Rousseau's thought on the social problem as developing in a context of other thought. It is concerned only with its nature and logic, with the way in which the argument unfolds and with the fundamental philosophical difficulties it involves. This argument I have abstracted from the more complex and confusing historical reality of Rousseau's thought. Such an abstraction may be in many respects a misleading picture of Rousseau. My claim is that it represents the central core of his thought on the individual and society.

2

NATURAL GOODNESS AND SOCIAL CORRUPTION

NATURE

The question that Rousseau undertook to answer in writing the *Discourse on the Origins of Inequality* was, what are the origins of inequality among mankind and is such inequality authorized by natural law? To answer this question Rousseau assumes that we have to know what the original condition of man was, so that we can trace from this starting point the development of inequality. He assumes therefore that this original condition was one of equality. He distinguishes between two sorts of inequality: on the one hand natural inequality, which consists in the differences created by nature between one person and another with regard to their qualities of body and mind; and on the other, what he calls moral or political inequality, arising out of some sort of convention, and consisting in the fact that some men are more rich, more honoured or more powerful than others.[1] Since the first sort of inequality is given by nature, we may say that Rousseau's assumption of original equality is the assumption that moral or political inequality does not form part of man's original condition, and thus its rise needs to be explained and to be justified.

Although the formal framework of the *Discourse* is provided by this question about inequality, Rousseau's concern is much wider, for it is directed at understanding the fundamental causes of the corruption which he takes to be deeply rooted in the way of life and consciousness of civilized social man. The question about inequality provides an entry into this wider enquiry, for he takes the presence of inequality, of the moral and political variety, to be intimately connected with the existence of corruption, so that an understanding of the rise of the one will provide an understanding of the rise of the other. Rousseau's concern to understand the causes or conditions of

[1] *The Political Writings of J. J. Rousseau*, ed. C. E. Vaughan (Oxford, 1962), vol. 1, p. 140. Unless otherwise stated all further page references in this chapter will be to the *Discourse on the Origins of Inequality* in vol. 1 of this edition. All translations in the chapter are my own.

the corruption of social man is not simply the concern of a disinterested enquirer after truth, for it arises also out of his desire to vindicate human nature against society, by showing that this corruption is not an inherent part of human nature, but rather the product of the social conditions in which man comes to exist. That man is naturally good is what he wishes to show and he thinks he can show this by explaining how from an original condition in which inequality and corruption are absent, both can be supposed to arise.

The initial aim of the enquiry is to arrive at a characterization of this original condition, the so-called state of nature, by which is meant a pre-social condition of man, in which the whole social context of historical man's life is assumed away, together with all those human characteristics that could have been acquired only in such a context. The result of the enquiry into the state of nature will provide the grounds to support the initial assumption that it is a state in which inequality and corruption are absent. This enquiry, however, will not be an historical one, and so the grounds provided will not be historical. About this Rousseau is clear, for he says that the state of nature is one 'which no longer exists, which has perhaps never existed, which probably never will exist, and yet of which it is necessary to have a clear idea in order to understand our present condition' (p. 136). If it is of no consequence whether the state of nature existed or not, what is an enquiry into it about? It is the exploration of an hypothetical idea which will enable us to say what can and cannot have been true of man's life and relations with others under the conditions posited. In Rousseau's case, what he hopes the exploration of the idea will enable him to say is that man in the conditions posited cannot have been subject to inequality and corruption, and cannot have been so subject for certain reasons. Understanding these reasons will help us to understand 'our present condition' whether or not man ever existed in a state of nature. The crucial question for Rousseau and for us then is what these reasons are.

The idea of a state of nature was not, of course, one that Rousseau invented nor was he unaware that his predecessors, notably Hobbes, had provided accounts of it which ran contrary to what he himself

6

wished to establish. In this respect he makes the general claim that while previous philosophers have investigated the state of nature, not one has properly arrived at it, for all have imported into their account characteristics or attributes of human life that could only have arisen and developed in a social context. Thus those who attribute to men in a state of nature notions of just and unjust, of property and authority, together with all those who talk of natural men as subject to passions of pride and desires of domination, have, he claims, taken their ideas of man in nature from man in society, and while talking of natural man, are describing civilized, social man (pp. 140–1). This, of course, is what he has to substantiate in his own account, but it indicates the way in which he is going to set about his task. If, to arrive at a proper understanding of man in a state of nature, we must assume away every aspect of human life that only makes sense in terms of men who possess social relations and institutions, then in dispossessing man of his social context we must suppose men and women to be living solitary and independent lives in primeval forests, meeting occasionally to satisfy their sexual needs and so reproduce the species, and otherwise haphazardly as they wander about the forests in search of their food and shelter. He then proceeds to give an account of what he thinks man's purely physical condition would be like in these circumstances, the details of which need not detain us, for they are only brought in to make the point that if man existed and survived in such a state, it would be reasonable to suppose that his physical characteristics were well adapted to the conditions of his existence.

Of more moment for Rousseau's enterprise is what he has to say about the moral or metaphysical side of natural man. He has already told us in the preface to the *Discourse* that in meditating upon the first and simplest operations of the human soul, he believes himself to have discerned two principles prior to the development of man's rational faculties; on the one hand a principle of self-preservation or self-love, which he calls *amour de soi*, and on the other a principle of pity, which he describes as involving a natural repugnance at seeing any sensitive being, but principally members of our own species, suffer or die (p. 138). These two principles he attributes to natural man, as being the fundamental determinants of his

7

behaviour. However, Rousseau also attributes both principles to animals, although pity of course in a very restricted degree, so that if we are concerned to distinguish natural man as distinctively human, albeit not social, neither of these principles will do the job for us. The life of natural man as so far presented to us, and given the above attributions to both men and animals, is hardly distinguishable from a possible life of solitary animals.

It is far from Rousseau's intention in depriving man of all his social characteristics to reveal him as in nature nothing but an animal, for in setting out to show man as naturally good and only corrupted in society, he has to show the being he describes as identifiably human. Otherwise he would deprive himself from the outset of a conception of human nature external to human nature in society, in terms of which the latter can appear as a corruption. He offers us two possible ways of distinguishing natural man from animals. The first is in terms of man's free agency. Every animal, he says, is an ingenious machine, to which nature has given senses to keep itself going, and to preserve itself from everything that tends to distort or destroy its existence. The same applies to the human machine, with this difference: that whereas nature alone governs every animal's activity, man contributes to the determination of his own in his capacity of free agent. This free agency manifests itself in man's capacity to will or choose independently of his natural impulses. It is, Rousseau says, in the consciousness of this liberty that the spirituality, or non-physical nature, of man's soul is displayed (p. 149), so that man even in nature is set apart from the natural world.

However, having offered us this, Rousseau immediately runs away from its implications, and because of the possible objections that might be made to the existence of free will, provides us with another way of distinguishing natural man from the animals, which he claims cannot be contested. This lies in the faculty of perfectibility, by which he understands a capacity in men to develop themselves, both individually and as a species, so that they change through time with the aid of changing circumstances in a way in which animals do not (pp. 149–50). What of course cannot be contested in this matter is the fact that men have so developed

8

themselves, and so must have had the capacity to do so. But in attributing this development to a special faculty that is not otherwise identified, or identifiable, Rousseau leaves us in total obscurity as to how it is that the development comes about, and so what it is in terms of men's characteristics that distinguishes them from animals.

The faculty of perfectibility explains nothing but merely points to facts, which from the standpoint of the original state of nature are not even present, but future. Nevertheless it provides an alternative to take us away from the first distinction offered, for the attribution of free will to natural man in the form described is not easily reconcilable with the other characteristics of natural man's life that Rousseau develops. For he wants to say of his natural man that he has through the simple impulses or instincts of nature all that is necessary for him to live well in the conditions he finds himself in, that is to be happy and contented with himself and all nature. Thus he distinguishes between two sorts of desires: on the one hand desires dependent on our having ideas or conceptions of the object desired; and on the other hand desires deriving directly from the impulses of nature. Rousseau takes the existence of desires of the former kind to depend on the development of man's rational faculty, which he claims is only latent in a state of nature. Thus natural man's desires being simply the instincts of nature will correspond to his physical needs, so that the only goods he knows are food, sex and sleep, and the only evils, hunger and pain (p. 151). He possesses neither imagination nor language, and having no understanding of past and future, lives only in the present. His behaviour in the present is governed by those two principles, *amour de soi* and pity, which themselves are impulses of the soul derived directly from nature, and not dependent on the existence of reason. In allowing himself to be guided by them, he follows instinctively what Rousseau calls the maxim of natural goodness, 'Pursue one's good with the least possible harm to others' (p. 163).

In so far then as natural man had, according to Rousseau, 'in instinct alone all that was necessary for him to live in the state of nature' (p. 159), free will would appear as an interruption of and potential interference with these natural impulses. For free will as described by Rousseau involves the capacity to distinguish oneself

9

from nature, and determine oneself to follow or not to follow nature's impulses. It is to be conscious of oneself as apart from nature, and of nature working on one. One would have to say, then, that natural man having free will always determines himself to act in virtue of a conscious decision to do or not to do something, and therefore not instinctively. Thus if natural man has in instinct alone all that is sufficient for him to lead a happy life, free will is certainly redundant, as having no function in such a life any more than reason has, but would also, if it occurred, be disruptive of the instinctive nature of that life.

If the faculty of perfectibility fails to distinguish anything in natural man that is not the animal man, since it only points to potential, not actual, differences, and free will, which in any case Rousseau is not keen to press, cannot be accommodated with the rest of Rousseau's account of natural man, then we appear to be left with no distinction at all between natural men and animals other than the former's stronger impulse of pity. Nevertheless while free will plays no further role in the argument, and indeed its role altogether is very unclear, there is a very important aspect in Rousseau's account of it, which recurs at later points as an unquestioned and undiscussed assumption, and which serves to show why Rousseau is not more particularly concerned with this problem. This aspect is the self-consciousness involved in free will, the consciousness of oneself as an individual set apart from the rest of the world, arising out of one's consciousness merely as subject to, but at the same time capable of resisting, the impulses of nature. Thus although free will as such disappears from the argument, this assumption of self-consciousness remains underlying Rousseau's presupposition that he is talking about a human animal, and not merely the animal species man.

In describing natural man as without reason, without language and without imagination, governed only by his limited physical needs and directed by the instinctive sentiments of *amour de soi* and pity, Rousseau would appear to have successfully assumed away everything that in being connected with human corruption in society could cause its existence in the state of nature. But this needs to be demonstrated. The crucial question concerns the struggle for existence. Rousseau is not assuming by his description of natural man's life as solitary and independent that those men are never in competition with each other for the objects of their desire. He specifically considers this question and argues that whenever such competition occurs, we must suppose it to be concerned with the immediate object of desire alone. When the decision is determined in favour of one contestant by force or the threat of force, the incident is immediately terminated, and from the point of view of both contestants forgotten (p. 163; see also notes on pp. 203, 217). That is to say, competition for objects of desire, even though settled by force, cannot lead to that state of war of every man against every man, which, according to Hobbes, characterizes man's natural condition. Rousseau's reasons for arguing thus are that on the one hand no passions are involved in the struggle other than the immediate desire for the object, and on the other that the natural fertility of unspoilt nature will ensure abundant occasion for the satisfaction elsewhere of the loser's desire. But if Rousseau is assuming that his men are not pressing on the margin of subsistence, this assumption is not of great importance relatively to the former. For even if we suppose that from time to time scarcity presented itself in an acute form, this would only lead to the periodic intensification of competition having the same nature as before, without that admixture of competitive passions which plays an essential role in Hobbes's deduction of perpetual war. So the central point is the argument about men's passions: what passions can coherently be said to be natural to man's existence?

In the main text of the *Discourse* Rousseau tells us that it is because men in nature have no settled relations with each other that they cannot be supposed to experience pride or vanity, esteem for others or contempt for others, or have any sense of what belongs to themselves or others, of mine and thine, of justice or of injury. Thus, although contests may involve violence, because neither pride nor desire for vengeance plays any part in the struggle, the contests will be limited to the immediate object of desire (p. 163). But this account in a way merely begs the question whether these passions are natural to man or not, whether they emerge with man's mere existence or only with his social existence. For it leaves unexplained why in the absence of settled relations men should not experience these passions. And in a very important note to the main text, Rousseau has a much more interesting account to give. In this passage he distinguishes between two sorts of self-love, *amour de soi*, which we have already met, and *amour-propre*. '*Amour de soi*', he says, 'is a natural sentiment, which leads every animal to concern itself with its own preservation, and which, directed in man by reason and modified by pity, produces humanity and virtue' (p. 217). On the other hand, '*amour-propre* is only a relative and factitious sentiment which is born in society, which leads each individual to make more of himself than of every other, which inspires in men all the evils they perpetrate on each other, and is the real source of the sense of honour' (p. 217). If it is *amour-propre*, as this socially created form of self-love, that engenders all the vicious and competitive passions that men experience, then, Rousseau claims, this *amour-propre* does not exist in a state of nature. For, he argues, it depends for its existence on the making by each individual of comparisons between himself and others, which natural man is not in a position to make. Hence Rousseau says:

This man could not experience either hate or desire for revenge, passions which can only grow from a sense of some offence given; and as it is the contempt or the intention to harm, and not the harm itself that constitutes the offence, men who do not know how to value or compare themselves with each other could do each other much violence, when occasion suited, without creating any offence. In a word, each man, more or less seeing his fellow men as he sees animals of another species, can seize the prey of a weaker man or surrender his own to a stronger, without seeing these acts of violence as other than natural events, without any element of insolence or spite, and without any other passion than the joy or grief of success or failure. (p. 217)

In this distinction between *amour de soi* and *amour-propre*, *amour de soi* must be understood as a form of self-love, in which the well-being of the self that is loved does not depend on how that self stands relatively to other selves and so on comparisons between one's own self and other selves, but only on how the self is absolutely for itself. *Amour propre* on the other hand must be understood as a form of self-love, in which the well-being of the self does depend on its standing relatively to other selves, and so on comparisons between itself and others. The vicious and competitive passions depend on *amour-propre* because they presuppose a consciousness in the self that is subject to these passions of relative status, which itself presupposes the making of comparative evaluations. If man in a state of nature is not in a position to make such comparisons, he cannot be supposed to love himself in the form of *amour-propre*, nor be subject to the vicious passions.

Whatever one assumes, then, about the scarcity of objects of desire in the state of nature, and the struggle between men for their acquisition, the competition cannot of itself engender the corrupt human passions, and Hobbes therefore must be wrong in attributing to man in nature a love of dominion over others. Natural men cannot on this argument be supposed to be dependent on each other, for they have neither the passions which could lead them to seek control or domination over others, nor the exchange or cooperative relations that could create an economic interdependence. They are on the contrary free beings in the sense of wholly independent, self-sufficient beings, meeting and clashing with each other only haphazardly and momentarily. There could in such circumstances be no sense either of property or of justice, but also no settled and acknowledged superiority of one man over another, establishing an inequality of rank or hierarchy. The only inequalities that could exist would be the inequalities of natural ability, as manifested in superior and inferior capacities in the struggle for existence. But differences so manifested will, Rousseau argues, in any case be minimal because of the uniformity in the conditions of existence that all men will experience (pp. 166–7), and could at the same time have no corrupting effect, because one man will see the superiority of another merely as a natural force to be contended with, like other natural forces, and not as an advantage which the other has over him in a competition for superior status.

Natural men, according to Rousseau, will be free, and, in all morally significant respects, equal beings, physically well adapted to their environment, and good in the sense that they are not subject to the corrupt and vicious passions of social man. They follow instinctively the maxim of natural goodness, formed out of the combination of the two fundamental principles of their souls, *amour de soi* and pity, and consisting in the pursuit of their own well-being with the least possible harm to others (p. 163). Given the self-sufficiency both of their material mode of existence and their consciousness, and the absence of the disturbing passions, such men cannot be supposed to be miserable or unhappy because there is nothing in their life which could be identified by them as constituting a defect which they could aspire to overcome (p. 158). Rousseau is, then, left with the problem of showing what changes must have occurred to wrest man from the peaceful and innocent slumber of his original condition, and turn him into a being for whom political order becomes a necessity. Since such changes, by the terms of his own argument, could not have come about through the development of human nature on its own, they must have occurred through external causes operating on man in such a way as to bring about the development of faculties latent within him, and so transform him into the corrupt social being of our own experience (p. 168). But before turning to a consideration of Rousseau's account of this transformation, I must take up again certain points in the preceding story which need closer attention, if we are to understand the full significance of the contrast and opposition that Rousseau draws between social and natural man.

The above account of natural man and his condition does not, as already indicated, serve to distinguish his existence from a purely animal existence, if we ignore free will and understand perfectibility as having future reference only. Man's natural goodness appears as nothing distinctively human, for it consists in the absence of those passions from which animals also are free. Everything Rousseau says of his natural man could equally well be said of animals, so that if nothing else is being implicitly assumed, his argument would have only this relevance to an understanding of the corruption of social man: that both man's humanity, whether this is understood in terms of free will or reason, perfectibility or morality, and man's corruption emerge only when the animal man becomes social; and this would not serve his purpose of showing social man as a corruption of a nature that is both human and good. But Rousseau quite certainly assumes that the man he is talking about is human, and although he has given us no clear reason for attributing humanity to him, never-

14

theless if we examine more closely what he implicitly assumes on occasion about his man, rather than what he explicitly says is distinctively human about him, we shall see why Rousseau is not more concerned that his man appears as nothing but an animal.

In the passage from which I have already quoted (above, p. 12) in which Rousseau distinguishes *amour de soi* from *amour-propre* in order to claim that *amour-propre* cannot exist in a state of nature, because men do not naturally compare themselves with one another, he offers as the reason for this fact the following consideration:

For since each man considers himself as the sole observer of himself, as the only being in the universe who takes any interest in him, as the sole judge of his own merit, it is impossible that a sentiment which depends on comparisons that he is not in a position to make could take root in his soul. (p. 217; my emphasis)

The passage emphasized clearly indicates that for Rousseau natural man possesses self-consciousness in the sense that he is not conscious simply of the world, but of himself as an individual agent in the world, and as such distinguished from the rest of the world. This is the same self-consciousness that is present in Rousseau's account of free will, where the agent is said to be conscious of himself as subject to and yet separated from nature, and so capable of acting with or against nature. Here it is the consciousness of his liberty that is said to manifest the spiritual nature of man's soul, and while the liberty drops out of the picture, self-consciousness appears to remain as what Rousseau implicitly assumes to characterize his natural man. That men are for themselves individuals in a way in which animals are not, through their being present to themselves in their consciousness, is an attribute of social man that distinguishes him from animals, and which Rousseau here is reading back into natural man without being clearly aware that he is doing it, and so of the importance of what he is doing.

Given that we are to understand Rousseau's natural man as having individuality for himself in the sense of possessing self-consciousness, certain complexities will now have to be introduced into the account that has so far been given of natural man's relations to his fellow men. The crucial element governing these relations for Rousseau was the existence of self-love in the form of *amour de soi* and not *amour-propre*. And the claim that *amour-propre* did not exist in a state of nature was based on the argument that *amour-propre* depends for its existence on comparisons that natural man is not in a position to make. This latter point however now ceases to be clear. For if natural man is capable of observing and judging himself, there seems to be no reason why he should not be in a position to compare himself with other men in respect of their physical capacities in the pursuit of existence. And indeed Rousseau says that natural men *will* make some comparisons, when confronted with the possibility of a contest with another over some object of desire. Before engaging in a fight they will compare the difficulty of winning with the opportunities of finding alternative satisfaction elsewhere (p. 203). To carry out such a comparison will involve the initial comparison between their own capacities and the capacities of the other.

The reason Rousseau offers for the inability of natural men to make comparisons between themselves and others is that each man sees himself as the sole observer and judge of himself. But an inability to make some sorts of comparisons clearly does not follow from this. What does follow, however, is that these comparisons cannot be such as to transform the nature of natural man's self-love into *amour-propre* and so engender the vicious and competitive passions. For in so far as each natural man sees himself as the sole observer and judge of himself, and sees other men 'almost as he sees animals of another species' (p. 217), he does not consider other men as being similar to himself in being endowed with an observing and critical consciousness. He cannot therefore see himself as being present to the consciousness of others and so having an individual existence for them. On the contrary, each natural man must exist for himself alone, not simply in the sense of his material independence, but also in the sense that the only consciousness in which he can consider himself to exist is his own. Other men must appear to him as alien and potentially hostile natural forces. Since natural man exists absolutely for himself alone, and other men as men like himself can have no meaning for him, he cannot have any concern for his standing relative to others, and so cannot love himself other than in the form of *amour de soi*. *Amour-propre*, as the form of self-love in which the well-being of the self depends on such relative standing, can have no influence on him, nor can he be affected by the vicious and competitive passions. The crucial point that Rousseau's position requires is not that natural man should be incapable of making comparisons, but that the comparisons he is in a position to make are made in a context in which each exists for himself alone as the only observing and judging consciousness in the world.[1]

The immediate significance of the above considerations concerns the nature of natural man's independence and self-sufficiency. For this might be thought of, from Rousseau's account, to consist simply in the fact that natural man has neither cooperative nor exchange relations with other men, but pursues his good in complete independence of them. But from the above considerations we can see that this independence is characterized also by the fact that each man is for himself the only human person in the world. Natural man is human in possessing individuality for himself, but this he possesses independently of the existence for him of any other human consciousness, so that his individual identity is determined for himself by himself alone without the intrusion of others on this identity. It is thus not beginning as a mere animal that natural man is to be developed by circumstances into civilized, social man, but as a being already inhabiting a human world, only a human world characterized by the existence of only one human being in it. The difficulties that, in Rousseau's story, subsequently beset this man will not, therefore, be understood, if they are conceived solely in terms of the contrast between material independence and material interdependence in his way of life, and it is not realized that they centre on the entrance into this human world of other human beings.

I have so far discussed Rousseau's account of natural man's life without saying anything about the role of pity in that life, other than to note Rousseau's attribution of it. Rousseau says of pity that it

---

[1] Of course it may be questioned whether it makes any sense to suppose that natural man could be in a position to observe and judge himself without being in a position to observe and judge others, whether he could have a notion of self without a notion of other selves. I do not pursue this, since the fundamental moral and social issues raised by Rousseau's argument can be considered independently of it.

serves to temper the ardour with which natural man pursues his own good, prevents him from depriving the young and the old of their subsistence, and generally ensures that he will follow the maxim of natural goodness by achieving his own good with the least possible harm to others (pp. 162–3). But Rousseau also says that it carries us without reflexion to the help of those we see suffer and that this involves putting ourselves in the place of the sufferer and identifying ourselves with him. This sentiment, leading us to identify with others is, he says, obscure in natural man. But it will nevertheless be stronger in him than in social man, for there will be no element of *amour-propre*, of competitive self-concern, to get in the way of this identification with the other (pp. 162–3). This pity, Rousseau also states here, is the basis for all subsequent social virtues, for what, he asks, are generosity, mercy, humanity, if they are not pity for the weak, the guilty and the human race in general (p. 161).

In view of the characterization of the nature of man's consciousness given above, this account of pity looks odd, for to identify oneself with the suffering other, would seem to require the recognition of the other as like oneself. But this possibility is just what is excluded by a consciousness which identifies other men not as like itself, but as another species of animal. Pity for men on the above account would have to involve the inclusion in a man's consciousness of other men as men and so destroy the isolated nature of his consciousness. Otherwise all we could attribute to natural man is a feeling for other men as suffering animals, which, although it might be supposed to involve an element of identification, could be no very intense emotion. It is also the case that, when Rousseau comes to discuss in *Emile* the emergence of pity and the importance of its role in the education of the sentiments, he describes pity as a relative sentiment, involving the comparison of oneself with others, and dependent on the imagination.[1] All these are characteristics that, in terms of the analysis of the *Discourse*, make pity into an unnatural sentiment, that is a sentiment which natural man could not be said to experience. Fundamentally this is so, because pity, even as described in the *Discourse*, and certainly as described in *Emile*, requires the ability to go out of oneself in one's feeling for the other,

[1] *Emile*, ed. Classiques Garnier (Paris, 1961), p. 261.

to live outside oneself in the other, whereas natural man is characterized as living wholly within himself, as exemplified in a consciousness which includes no others in it.

This problem regarding the status of pity in Rousseau's thought
about man is not simply a little local difficulty, for it is a source of
Rousseau's later important ambiguities. As presented here in the
Discourse pity not only has the role of underlining man's natural
goodness, but also, in being said to be the source of all social virtues,
serves to indicate that, at least in this respect, man has a natural
capacity for communal living. For in so far as the character of
natural man is predominantly given by the nature of his self-love, he
is essentially self-dependent, a being whose nature it is to live for
itself alone; so that unless Rousseau wishes to maintain the position
that society in itself, and so society even at its best, is contrary to
human nature, which he does not wish to say unambiguously, he
must find something in human nature which constitutes a capacity
for social living, for living for others as well as for himself, and this
role he gives to pity. But to the extent that the sentiment of pity is
out of character with the rest of man's natural consciousness, pity as a
natural sentiment is called into question. It is redescribed more
convincingly in *Emile* in such a way as to bring out its 'unnatural'
features. But since pity is presented by Rousseau as the solution to
the social problem, and since this solution is claimed to be founded
on man's nature, the solution itself is called into question.

SOCIETY

Man in his original condition, devoid of language, rationality and
morality, but free, equal and individually self-sufficient, had no
cause either in the conditions of his existence or in his nature to seek
to associate with other men as an improvement on or remedy for
deficiencies in his mode of life. So some story needs to be given of
his departure from this happy, if stupid, condition, and of the
emergence of society and creation of social man, which represents it
not as the potentially conscious construction of men, but as something that happened to them as a consequence of other changes. The
changes, Rousseau says, that he is going to give an account of could

have occurred in various ways, so that his actual story is to be taken as conjectural. Nevertheless, what is important are the consequences he deduces from the changes that he posits, and these consequences, he claims, are not conjectural, for given his initial starting point, described above, any other possible story must yield exactly the same conclusions (p. 168). It is not the detailed process of change that is important, so much as the character of the end state of this process, namely society and social man. That is to say, since we now know the initial condition, man as self-sufficient, living entirely for himself, and since we also know the general outlines of the concluding position, man as dependent being, having to be concerned for others as well as himself, we can fill in the intervening stages in various ways without seriously affecting our understanding of the concluding position. This understanding is an understanding of the sort of transformation that must have occurred in man's nature and consciousness attendant upon his emergence as dependent social being, and will be the same whatever intervening stages we posit.

The story Rousseau tells can be given very briefly and includes the following elements: as the human race increased in numbers and spread over the earth, men began to develop different modes of maintaining themselves according to the differences of their locations; they developed tools and skills of one sort or another to suit their circumstances; in beginning to experiment, they began to acquire understanding of relations between one being and another; and they came to see other members of their species as beings similarly endowed to themselves. They started cooperating with one another from time to time on enterprises such as hunting expeditions. They constructed permanent shelters or dwelling places and came to live in families; and language developed. Once families had made their appearance and become fixed in permanent locations, relations between neighbouring families were constituted, and out of the constant communication carried on between such families individuals began to acquire a special identity and preference for each other, and the basis of a loose and primitive society was created.

At this point Rousseau has the following passage:

As ideas and feelings progressed, and the mind and the heart were exercised, men continued to become less wild; their connexions with each

other became more binding as they developed. They accustomed themselves to assemble before their huts or around a large fire; singing and
dancing, true off-spring of love and leisure, became the amusement or
rather the occupation of men and women thus idly gathered together.
Each one began to consider the rest and to wish to be considered in turn,
and public esteem came to acquire a value. Whoever sang or danced the
best, whoever was the most handsome, the strongest, the most skilful, or
the most eloquent, came to be of most consideration; and this was the
first step towards inequality and vice at the same time. From these first
distinctions arose on the one side vanity and contempt, on the other shame
and envy; and the fermentation caused by these new germs finally produced compounds fatal to innocence and happiness. (p. 174)

The transformation of man's nature and consciousness from its
original to its social constitution is here first introduced and a crucial
element in the process, which is finally fatal to human happiness and
innocence, is that men should come to have for themselves, not as in
Rousseau's state of nature a purely private identity, but a public
identity, the identity created for them by public opinion to which
they attach value. Whereas in nature man existed for himself alone,
in the sense that how he was for himself depended only on his
own consciousness of himself, what happens on this view with the
emergence of the most primitive forms of society is that men, having
begun to value others, acquire the desire to be valued by them, and
so become concerned with the identity they have in the eyes of
others. That this involves the first step towards inequality is because
the concern for one's identity for others is at the same time a concern
to be distinguished as superior. The arrival of vice on the scene as
well can only be because the nature of man's self-love has been transformed from *amour de soi* into *amour-propre*. Men must have come to
identify the self that they love, and so its well-being, in terms of this
new public identity constituted by their existence for others, so that
each becomes dependent for his happiness on the relative standing
he acquires in the opinion of others. For the peculiarly human vices
that Rousseau refers to, the passions which inflame men against each
other, depend for their existence on a man's self-love taking the form
of *amour-propre*, since they all presuppose that the individual's
primary self-identification is in terms of his appearances for others.

While *amour-propre* thus emerges with the earliest forms of social relations, and consequently creates a competitive and potentially vicious element in human intercourse, which was hitherto lacking, we are nevertheless only at the foundation of the movement that constitutes man's progressive corruption. Thus although at this point men are on their guard in their relations with each other in respect of their mutual appreciation and evaluation, so that 'every intended injury becomes an outrage, because the injured feels in it not simply the harm but the contempt of his person' (p. 174), and men become vengeful, bloody and cruel, Rousseau nevertheless claims that this primitive social condition 'was the least subject to radical change, the best for man, and one which he should never have left but for some fatal chance which for the common good should never have occurred' (p. 175). In this happiest condition of men human faculties have been developed only to an extent which preserves a just mean between the indolence of the original state and the petulant activity of the *amour-propre* which characterizes more sophisticated social man. But Rousseau tells us little about this golden age, other than that in it men, or rather families, are economically independent of each other, having limited needs, which they can satisfy themselves without becoming dependent on the activities of others, and so live free, healthy, good and happy lives within the limits of their modified nature, and enjoying the pleasures of an independent intercourse.

It might be thought that this primitive social condition, since Rousseau sees it as a sort of golden age, plays an important role in his thought about social man. And it is true that something of the same idea, that is of economically self-sufficient families enjoying an independent, i.e. non-essential, intercourse with each other, recurs from time to time in his various writings as an ideal human existence. It is an existence which is clearly both human and social, and yet at the same time lacks most of the corrupting and competitive pressures of society associated with the activity of our *amour-propre* and the dependence of men on each other. But while it is an ideal to be longed for and which may yet be realized by a few fortunately placed individuals, as a general arrangement for mankind its relevance disappeared long ago with the 'fatal chance' that caused men to bring about the changes which destroyed that existence. What this

ideal represents, then, a form of social existence with minimal corruption because there is no economic interdependence and other social
relations of an infrequent and non-necessary nature, in short the
simple, self-sufficient peasant life, has no bearing on the substance of
Rousseau's argument, for this argument concerns the options for
men, who, in becoming dependent on and necessary for each other,
confront the conditions of maximum corruption.

What destroys this golden age is, according to Rousseau, the
invention of the arts of metallurgy and agriculture, the development
of the latter being dependent on the discovery of the former. It is
the invention of metallurgy that is represented as the product of
some fatal chance, for Rousseau supposes that the working of iron
could only have come about as the result of some extraordinary
circumstance, such as a volcanic eruption, which, in vomiting metals
in fusion, suggested to men the idea of imitating this operation of
nature. But however Rousseau thinks this came about, it is the
consequences of these changes that are important, and these are
specialization, division of labour, exchange of products, and thus
economic interdependence. At the same time, as a result of the
development of agriculture, private property comes into existence,
and with it the first rules of justice. It is at this point, Rousseau says,
that equality disappears, that original equality that had been maintained into the golden age because of the limitations on production
arising out of the self-sufficiency of each family. But with the development of specialization, exchange and private property, these limitations are removed, and because of the inequality in men's talents,
which results in the stronger, the more skilful and the more inventive
accumulating more than others, the natural differences between
men, developed by circumstances, come to have more permanent
effects and begin to determine the lot of individuals.

From this initial impetus everything else develops: the other arts,
the progress of language, the inequality of fortunes, the uses and
abuses of riches, and it is only at this point that the rest of men's
faculties, passions and vices are provided with the opportunity for
their full development.

Here then are all our faculties developed, memory and imagination in
play, *amour-propre* involved, reason become active and mind arrived

already at almost the final perfection it is capable of. Here then are all man's natural qualities displayed, the rank and lot of each man established, not only in respect of fortune and the ability to serve and harm others, but in respect of intelligence, beauty, strength and skill, merit and talents; and these qualities, being the only ones which could gain a man the consideration of others, it was soon necessary to have or to affect them; it was necessary for one's advantage to display oneself as other than one in effect was. Being and appearance became two completely different things; and from this distinction emerged ostentation designed to impose on others, deceitful trickery and all the vices that follow in their train. (p. 178)

From a naturally free and independent being man has become, through the creation of a multitude of new needs, subject to all of nature, but above all to his fellow men, of whom he becomes the slave even in becoming their master. For all are dependent on each other, the rich on the poor, as well as the poor on the rich, not only for necessary economic services, but because the desire for, and attraction of, riches does not consist in their power to satisfy real need, but in the superiority they give the rich over other men (p. 179). The rich only value their possessions to the extent that others are deprived of them, and, without changing their condition, would cease to be happy if the poor ceased to be miserable (p. 192). Society is thus characterized by a pervasive competition and rivalry, the opposition of interests, and always the hidden desire to make one's profit at the expense of others. All these evils, Rousseau says, are the first effect of property, and the inseparable consequence of growing inequality.

From here Rousseau continues the story of man's progressive degeneration in terms of the increasing disorders that result from the creation of classes of rich and poor, until political society with its legal structure and clearly defined authority is invented by the rich as an attempt to legitimize and stabilize the superior positions they had achieved, but which were continuously threatened by the depredations of the propertyless and expropriated poor. Thus political society is created as a response to disorders that are the product of an already social situation, and not to disorders inherent in human nature. Although this new order is represented as a device by the rich to secure their position, this depends on its legitimation and thus on the endorsement by the poor of the new arrangements. What the poor are offered, and believe they will gain from, is a system of equal rights and duties which will guarantee everybody in his life and property from the invasions of others (p. 181). But in fact, Rousseau says, they gain nothing, and only lose their natural liberty (p. 183). While Rousseau does not develop this statement, the implication is that to the extent that the political and legal order is imposed on a social situation in which the rich dominate the poor, the equality of rights and duties that it proclaims is a fraud. Equality is offered but the social situation renders it nugatory. But, as I said, these thoughts are not developed, and Rousseau goes on to give an account of the various changes that will afflict the body politic, until it finally arrives at the extreme point of human inequality and corruption, the subjection of all to the arbitrary and despotic will of the tyrant. But what Rousseau has to say about these changes I will not enter into, for they merely continue the story of inequality and corruption, without in any way modifying or developing the essential argument about human nature and human society that is contained in the *Discourse*. For as he says:

If this were the place to enter into details, I would easily explain how, without any intervention from government, inequality of consideration and authority becomes inevitable between individuals, so soon as gathered together in a single society they are forced to compare themselves with each other, and to pay attention to the differences which manifest themselves through the continual use they make of one another. (p. 191)

The essence of the problem is generated not by politics but by society independent of politics, and the political order appears here in the *Discourse* as merely a palliative measure designed to favour the party of the rich while leaving untouched the central issue. What is untouched by politics is the new social consciousness men have acquired, which must now be more closely examined.

The transformation of human nature into a potentially corrupt and vicious thing was seen to occur, together with the earliest societies, with the emergence of a new consciousness involving *amour-propre* as its fundamental principle. However, Rousseau immediately redescribed these earliest societies as constituting a golden age for man, and subsequently attributed the evils of the social condition to the creation of private property, and the growing inequality between rich and poor, itself dependent on changes in the modes of production bringing about economic interdependence, specialization and exchange. Thus if one does not attend closely to Rousseau's argument, one gains the impression that the fundamental trouble is simply private property and this class division between rich and poor. But in the context of Rousseau's whole argument the sense in which all evils are attributed to property and economic inequality can only be that these latter create the conditions and constitute the materials for the burgeoning of an evil that had already made its appearance in the golden age. Property and economic inequality merely provide the fertile soil for *amour-propre*, hitherto restricted in its growth by the egalitarian circumstances of primitive social man's existence, to spring into vigorous life. That is to say, it is not the class division between rich and poor that of itself produces the evil, but only in so far as this division appears in a context in which men are already potentially corrupt, by already depending for their self-satisfaction on the status they have in the eyes of others. Wealth is desired for the superior condition it affords, and for the other superiorities that through it can be acquired or affected. The ultimate cause of all the trouble is *amour-propre* which brings it about that men are concerned not with how they are with themselves, but with how they are seen by others, and inequality of property and wealth is only the immediate cause as constituting the conditions necessary for the manifestation of the full effectiveness of the ultimate cause.

The fact that it is ultimately to moral and not to economic causes that Rousseau attends in his interpretation of the social problem is clearly brought out in the following passages, the first of which is the continuation of the passage quoted immediately above in which he tells us in brief what he says he would tell us at length if it were the place:

I would remark how much the universal desire of reputation, honours and precedence, which devours all of us, exercises and compares our talents and capacities; how much it excites and multiplies the passions; and how much, by turning all men into competitors, rivals or rather enemies, it brings about every day, reverses, successes and catastrophes of every kind, by making so many pretenders engage in the same race. I would show how it is to this passion to have oneself spoken of, this fury to distinguish oneself, which keeps us almost always outside ourselves, that we owe what is best and worst among men: our virtues and vices, our science and our errors, our conquerors and philosophers; that is to say a multitude of bad things together with a small number of good. (p. 192)[1]

In the second passage he is concluding the *Discourse* with a contrast between the spirit of natural man on the one hand and sophisticated social man on the other, in order to bring out to what extent the latter had become an artificial creation of the new relations he has entered into, and not at all the product of nature. Natural man breathes only the spirit of repose and liberty, and is profoundly indifferent to every other object; and if he is to understand the agitated and tormented life of social man, Rousseau says:

It would be necessary that these words, *power* and *reputation*, have meaning for him; and that he learns that there is a sort of men who value the opinion of the rest of the world, who are happy and content with themselves on the testimony of others rather than on their own. This is in effect the true cause of all these differences: the savage lives within himself; social man, always outside himself, knows how to live only in the opinions of others; and it is, so to speak, from their judgement alone that he derives the sense of his own existence. (p. 195)

If the true cause of all the differences between natural and social man is that the latter lives outside himself in the opinions of others, this presupposes that the fundamental principle of social man's actions has become *amour-propre*. What Rousseau is saying about the social condition of corruption, then, is that men become dependent on each other, not simply economically, but for their identities for themselves, their sense of their own existence and their happiness, so that they become the creature of others rather than, as in nature, their own self-creation. This dependence on others involves the transformation of a man's self-love from the solely self-referring *amour de soi* into the relative and other-dependent *amour-propre*, and this itself involves the emergence of an intense competitiveness in men's relations arising out of the need, in order to be well with themselves, to achieve superiority over others. If this is the condition

---

[1] The reference in this passage to the good things produced by this movement of the self is not followed up in the *Discourse*, so I here also ignore its implications.

of corruption, I shall now examine more closely what Rousseau is saying about how this condition comes into existence and what its implications are.

In the first place it may look as though for Rousseau social man is irremediably corrupt. For in so far as this corruption is identified with social man's coming to an awareness of his existence for others, and his coming to depend for his own identity and happiness on this existence, there appears no possible alternative mode of social life which can avoid this state. The ideal of the golden age, which is in any case by now irrelevant, itself endorses this view, since it reduces the level of corruption only by reducing social relations to a harmless minimum and thus reveals how, for Rousseau, the extent of corruption is tied to the extent and intensity of social relations. There appears to be no way of enjoying the society of others without corrupting oneself and others. And it is true that in Rousseau's subsequent writings, this negative revulsion from society in general recurs, and the good man is conceived of mechanically as he who has the fewest social relations;[1] nevertheless, both *Emile* and the *Social Contract* are attempts to conceive of a type of social consciousness and a type of society which, while not eradicating the ever-present potential for corruption, at least show what a non-corrupt social existence would be like. If this reformation of social man, this posited creation of a new social man, is not to contradict the argument of the *Discourse*, it must be possible to see in this argument the roots of potential reform.

The state of corruption for Rousseau is identified in terms of this living outside oneself in the opinions of others by which one becomes dependent on them, together with the competitive consciousness and competitive relations associated with it, and the question I shall now consider in more detail is how exactly according to Rousseau this corrupt state comes about. In the first passage in which this corrupting *amour-propre* is referred to (see above, p. 12), Rousseau claimed that natural men were not in a position to compare themselves with one another and hence could not experience *amour-propre*. As I showed there, this statement was not fully coherent, and what he should have said to make more sense, both in the immediate

[1] For example see *Emile*, note to p. 99.

and more general context of his argument, was that it was the fact that natural men were not aware of being present to the conscious-ness of others that rendered any comparisons they were in a position to make irrelevant from the point of view of potential corruption. The passage implied, however, that it is the making of comparisons between oneself and others that creates the radical break between nature and society, and between a natural and social consciousness. This idea is maintained in Rousseau's account of the generation of corruption in the second part of the *Discourse*. In the passage already quoted (see above, pp. 20–1), which is in effect the only description Rousseau gives of the actual process of psychological transformation that man experiences in society, he says that when men began to associate in common activities, such as singing and dancing, 'each one began to consider the rest and to wish to be considered in turn, and public esteem came to acquire a value'. What this implies is that the process of transformation begins in each individual's separate consciousness and evaluation of others as good singer, dancer and so on, which then brings about a desire on his part to be appreciated as such by others in his turn. Hence the opinions of others become important for him, and he comes to have and desire for himself a public identity. In this account the public identity and the living in the opinions of others, which is the constituent element in the condition of corruption, comes about as a result of a process which begins with the individual's evaluation of others, and compari-son of his own performances with theirs.

In another passage, again already quoted (see above, p. 25), the same implication, that it is the comparing oneself with others that is fundamental in the social transformation of man, occurs, but not so clearly. Here he says that inequality of consideration and auth-ority becomes inevitable, 'so soon as [men] gathered together in a single society . . . are forced to compare themselves with each other'. While it is inequality and not the living in the opinions of others that is said to follow from the making of comparisons, it seems reasonable to suppose, in view of the fact that the passage continues with an account of the effects of men's desire to be distinguished in the opinions of others, that he is taking, here also, the making of com-parisons to be the fundamental point of departure for the generation of both inequality and corruption. Only in saying that men are 'forced' to make comparisons he suggests a further cause which he does not mention.

Apart from the two passages quoted above Rousseau's account of the corrupt social condition does not specify what comes first as the generative element in the process. Nevertheless it is important to try and get a clear idea of what he is assuming and also of the adequacy of these assumptions, in order to understand the terms in which the social problem for man presents itself to Rousseau at the end of the *Discourse*. For these terms determine also the possibilities that remain for the conception of a reformed state of man and society, and thus give us an initial entry into the problems with which Rousseau is concerned in *Emile* and the *Social Contract*.

What Rousseau seems to be saying is that it is in the first place the making of comparative evaluations of each other which psychologically marks the break between natural and social men; that these comparative evaluations create in men a desire to be distinguished in the opinions of others and thus at the same time both a concern for their relative status and a dependence for their self-identity on how they exist in the eyes of others; and finally that this transformation engenders a fundamentally competitive consciousness in men, which is reflected in equally competitive and vicious relations between them.

But as I have already argued this cannot be a completely satisfactory account. It must be the case that, at the point at which men begin to make the comparative evaluations they are already aware of having an individual existence in each other's consciousness, and importance is attached to this identity they have for others. This is obvious in the story that Rousseau gives us about singing and dancing. If, as a result of making comparative evaluations of each other in the context of their association in these common activities, men desire to be distinguished in the opinions of others, and so become concerned with their public identity and relative status, it is obvious in the conditions posited of mutual acquaintance and association that they are already aware of having individual identities for each other which they value. But one can say also that it must necessarily be the case that this existence and importance for each other precedes the desire to be distinguished in the opinion of others and the competitive concern for relative status. For the desire to be distinguished can only be supposed to arise in individuals if they are already aware of having an identity for others which is important for them. It is the making of comparative evaluations in a situation in which men already exist for each other and attach importance to this existence that makes sense of the emergence of a competitive concern for relative status and the state of corruption that Rousseau describes.

I thus take Rousseau to be quite right in emphasizing the making of comparative evaluations as the point of departure for the process of corruption, only the point I am making is that the break with the natural condition of man's consciousness must have occurred already for these comparative evaluations to have their corrupting effects. Men must have ceased already to exist for themselves alone, and have become concerned with their existence for others in a way which supposes a certain degree of dependence on them for the identity they give themselves – a certain degree, that is, of living outside themselves in the consciousness of others. It is indeed in terms of the opposition between living in oneself alone and living outside oneself in others that Rousseau distinguishes the life of natural man from that of corrupt social man. But he seems to understand the latter as arising out of the making of comparative evaluations, and this I claim must be false.

If we now ask the question: what possibilities, in view of all this, present themselves for a conception of a reformed state of social man?, we would have to say that any such conception must start from an understanding of the irreversible break with nature occurring at the level of consciousness in this awareness and concern for one's existence for others. Any new social consciousness must at least presuppose this, so that the possibilities for a reformed social man must involve an existence for others which yet excludes corruption. What, then, has got to be excluded in order to exclude corruption? Obviously the initial priority is the competitive concern for relative status, so that the real problem is to determine what has to be excluded to exclude this. Since it is quite clearly the making of comparative evaluations that generates the competitive self-concern, it would seem that it is these that would have to be excluded. But since these comparative evaluations are identified by Rousseau with the initial creation of a social consciousness and so with the irreversible break with nature, this does not seem a possibility open to Rousseau. The other alternative for exclusion is the dependence on others that is involved in living outside oneself in the opinions of others. If there could be conceived a form of social consciousness and a form of social existence which destroyed this dependence, it would also appear to carry with it the destruction of competitive self-concern. For if one's identity in the eyes of others ceased to have a determining influence on one's own identity for oneself, this would seem to remove the basis of a meaningful concern for one's relative status. Since it is indeed this dependence on others that Rousseau, in the *Discourse*, but also in his later writings, consistently identifies as the true cause of corruption, the possibilities open to him for a new conception of social man, arising out of the terms of his analysis of the social problem in the *Discourse*, would appear to be restricted to the conception of a way in which men could make comparisons of one another which did not generate a dependence on each other and so a competitive consciousness.

But we can immediately see in terms of my critique of Rousseau's analysis that such a programme would seem to be an impossible undertaking. For if an awareness of existing for others must be a constituent element in any social consciousness, Rousseau's programme would involve preventing this awareness from expressing itself in a concern for the identity one has for others, and so in an other-dependent consciousness. This would require an awareness that was accompanied by a denial of the importance to oneself of others as centres of consciousness in which one exists. Otherwise their importance for one will be reflected in a certain degree of dependence on them. And while this rejection of others is a possible attitude, it does not appear to be a conceivable basis for a reformed social and political morality.

Nevertheless this is what, as I shall attempt to show below, Rousseau undertakes to do, and is the ultimate reason why the enterprise cannot succeed and must be incoherent. For it involves the attempt to conceive of a social consciousness which is both a moral consciousness and also preserves the stance of natural man, a stance

32

in which each exists for himself alone in his own consciousness and his individual existence for others has no importance for him. In being a moral consciousness it must assert the importance of others, but in being a consciousness which excludes dependence on others, it must at the same time deny the importance of others. This incoherence is reflected in the lack of clarity in Rousseau's account in *Emile* and the *Social Contract* of what is supposed to be happening to nature. For society is to be refounded on nature to avoid the wrong turning taken by the social men of the *Discourse*, and yet the nature which is to serve as the new foundation involves an essentially non-social consciousness which has to be destroyed for society to emerge. Thus we will find in Rousseau's conception of a reformed social condition the requirement that the new social relations preserve nature and that they completely destroy it.

It is important to note at this point that when Rousseau identifies living in the opinions of others as a constituent element of the corrupt consciousness, he does not distinguish different degrees of such living, and so does not distinguish different degrees of dependence. Or rather the degree of dependence is related only to the extent and intensity of social relations: the less these are, the less will this dependence be. He does not allow, that is to say, for the way in which in the normal case a due concern for the opinions of others is mediated in the individual's self-conception by his own judgement, so that the individual remains judge of himself even while attending to the judgements of others. He presents the concern for the opinions of others as though this involved the complete abnegation of the individual's self-judgement, and so appears to leave us with the choice between complete determination by others or complete self-determination, between an unqualified dependence and an unqualified independence. But it is only in the extreme and abnormal case, involving extreme weakness of character, that a man in submitting to be judged by others accepts without mediation the conception of him that others have. Since this is not normally the case, whether dependence, characterized as the concern for one's appearances for others, is corrupting or not might be found to depend on the degree to which the individual's own self-judgement is developed and preserved, and so on the balance achieved between

33

his own judgement and that of others, a balance, that is to say, between dependence and independence. In treating dependence as without qualification corrupt and corrupting, any such possibility is excluded for Rousseau, and we are left with either total dependence or total independence.

Before leaving the *Discourse* we must consider what Rousseau's conclusions are about equality and inequality. What he called at the beginning of the *Discourse* moral or political inequality, to distinguish it from natural inequality, was seen to emerge in two ways. In the first place in relation to the carrying on of common activities, in which some men manifest and are judged by others to possess superior capacities to others, an inequality of status results. In the second place an inequality of wealth develops out of the opportunities provided by the creation of an economy involving specialization and exchange for the more skilful, inventive and hard-working to accumulate more than others. This inequality of condition affects inequalities of status, in so far as the richer have more opportunities to develop their talents, or otherwise supplement their lack of them by what wealth can buy or put on. Rousseau concludes the *Discourse* with the statement to the effect that moral inequality is only legitimate in so far as it corresponds to natural inequality (p. 196), and this conclusion seems clear enough. Nevertheless, in relation to the whole preceding argument, it is not without its difficulties, which we may briefly consider. Thus, inequalities of status, whether justified or not in terms of natural inequalities, arise out of and are dependent on the corrupting spirit of society. For it is only when men become concerned with how they appear to others that the sorts of judgements can be attended to that create at the same time both status and inequalities of status. This spirit of society, however, creates not only the possibility of inequality of status, but through *amour-propre*, its directing principle, engenders a love of it in the form of *amour-propre*'s desire for superiority over others: so that inequality of status appears as the source and object of all social disorders. If, therefore, a new consciousness is to replace the old, it would seem to have at the same time to do away with the conditions that make moral or political inequality both possible and desired.

34

Natural goodness and social corruption

But this, as it will appear, becomes not a mere by-product of other concerns, but itself a moral necessity, and the love of equality will emerge as a principle of the new social consciousness, as the love of inequality was a principle of the old.

3

THE NEW MAN

THE PROJECT DEFINED

My analysis of the *Discourse* left Rousseau with a radical opposition between nature and society, between on the one hand man's natural condition, in which he lives for himself absolutely without reference to others, and on the other his actual social condition, in which, coming to live for himself as he exists for others, he degenerates, his original nature and goodness are stifled through the creation of the false spirit of society, and he ceases to be good for himself without becoming good for others. The problem with which this opposition presents Rousseau is how, if we can neither return to nature in its original form, nor be content with our present corrupt social existence, we can reform social man in such a way as to bring about a reconciliation between nature and society. The programme that Rousseau develops in response to this problem is worked out on two levels: on the one hand in *Emile* in the form of a moral education for the new man, and on the other hand the elucidation in the *Social Contract* of the political principles that should govern the new society. Thus *Emile*, with which I am here immediately concerned, is an attempt to deal with the problem, by giving an account of an education designed to be in accordance with man's nature, but nevertheless fitting him for the society of others, so that through the creation of a new social consciousness, man can become good for others, while remaining, as in nature, good for himself. The new man is to be natural man educated to live in cities.[1]

Although I thus assume that Rousseau's twofold programme is aimed at developing the same sort of answer, but at different levels, to the same problem, and consequently that the two parts should be fully coherent with one another, nevertheless in the opening pages of *Emile* Rousseau makes a distinction which appears immediately to call this assumption into question by reformulating the idea of the

---

[1] *Emile*, ed. Classiques Garnier (Paris, 1961), p. 240. Unless otherwise stated all further page references in this chapter are to this edition. All translations in the chapter are my own.

opposition between nature and society. He distinguishes between two sorts of education that it is possible to give men: a public or communal education on the one hand, and a private or domestic one on the other. The ends of these two types of education, Rousseau says, are entirely different and indeed contradictory, for the latter aims to bring up a man to live for himself, while the concern of the former is to educate a man to live for others. The one is a development of nature and repudiates the requirements of society, while the other accepts the demands of society and repudiates nature.

Compelled to combat either nature or social institutions, one must choose between making a man or making a citizen: for one cannot make both at the same time. (p. 9)

And he goes on to explain why this is so:

Natural man exists entirely for himself; he is the numerical unity, the absolute whole, who relates only to himself or to another like him. The citizen is only a fraction which depends on the denominator and the value of which consists in its relation to the whole, which is the social body. Good social institutions are those which know best how to denature man, remove from him his absolute existence, in order to give him a relative one, and to transport the 'I' into the communal unity; in such a way that each particular no longer thinks himself to be a unity, but part of one, and feels himself to exist only in the whole. (p. 9)

The opposition that is drawn in these passages between nature and society, man and citizen, is however not identical with the opposition drawn in the same terms in the *Discourse* and referred to immediately above. The citizen of these passages, who has to have his original nature destroyed in order to exist relatively to a whole larger than himself, is not at all the same as the degenerate social man of the *Discourse*. For that man, driven by *amour-propre*, was still concerned to exist as an individual identity for himself, but to exist as this at the same time for others, while the true citizen, as described here, appears to be required to destroy this individuality in himself altogether by existing only as member of a larger whole. Degenerate social man appears rather in a passage immediately following the above, thus:

He who wishes to preserve the primacy of the natural sentiments in the social order does not know what he wishes. Always in contradiction with himself, always wavering between his inclinations and his duties, he will never be either a man or a citizen; he will be neither good for himself nor for others. He will be one of our contemporary men, a Frenchman, an Englishman, a bourgeois: he will be nothing. (p. 10)

The social man of the *Discourse*, unlike the true citizen in whom original nature must be entirely destroyed, is still in a sense the product of nature, for he wants to preserve what he is by nature, his being for himself an individual identity, and yet in trying at the same time to be this for others, he contradicts this original nature, and thereby ceases to be anything significant at all. For, Rousseau says:

To be something, to be oneself and always a unity, one must act as one speaks: one must always be resolved on the role one must take, take it nobly, and follow it always. I await to be shown this prodigy to know whether he is man or citizen, or how he manages if he is at the same time the one and the other. (p. 10)

While social man of the *Discourse* tries to exist both for himself and for others, and is consequently a self-contradictory nullity, both natural man and the true citizen, because the one lives entirely for himself and the other entirely for others, achieve a significant unity in their lives, and so become something. Thus although there is a radical opposition between what it is to be a man and what it is to be a citizen, the ways of life they involve are both in a sense valid in so far as in themselves they constitute coherent forms of existence. Both have value in contrast to the incoherence and self-contradictoriness of the life of degenerate bourgeois social man.

We have here a twofold opposition between nature and society: in the first place the one arising out of the argument of the *Discourse*, and secondly a new one consisting in this novel conception of social man as totally denatured citizen, who nevertheless achieves an existence to which value is attributed. It is the first opposition that remains as the social problem to be overcome, but we are now presented with the idea of two possible solutions to it, neither of which appears immediately as a solution at all. For the one is said to develop nature while ignoring the requirements of society, and the other produces a citizen in whom no element of nature remains. They appear as intended solutions to something, but not to the problem as initially presented. Whatever they are intended as solutions to, it is still the case that we appear to have to choose between them, and since the conception of citizenship presented here points forward to the solution contained in the political principles of the *Social Contract*, *Emile*, as representing the natural solution, and the *Social Contract*, as the solution against nature, cannot form, it would appear, part of the same programme.

Nevertheless they do, for despite these introductory oppositions Rousseau immediately goes on to say that perhaps the objects of the two sorts of education, producing a man and producing a citizen, may after all be reconcilable with each other.

There remains finally domestic education or the education of nature, but what will a man become for others, who is educated uniquely for himself? If perhaps, the double object proposed [man and citizen] could be reunited in one single object, one would, in removing the contradictions in man, have removed a large impediment to his happiness. It would be necessary to decide this question to see him fully formed; it would be necessary to observe his inclinations, his progress, to follow his steps; it would be necessary in a word to know natural man. (p. 11)

And the rest of *Emile* is the carrying through of this proposal to get to know natural man, by the demonstration of what an education according to nature involves, and how the product of such an education, namely Emile, the new man, will not only be capable of taking his place as citizen in a true republic, but will be supremely fitted for such citizenship, and in doing so will have become what Rousseau has already said is impossible, at the same time and without contradiction good both for himself and others, both man and citizen.

We can consequently now revert tentatively, in accordance with Rousseau's tentativeness, to my original formulation of Rousseau's problem and programme. The problem is the reconciliation of nature and society, and the programme to resolve the opposition between them, first in terms of a moral education, and secondly in terms of the political principles proper for a reformed communal life. But we can present the problem rather more clearly as the attempt to conceive of a form of social life which avoids the self-contradictoriness of the corrupt bourgeois form by showing how the life of man according to nature and the life of the citizen can be reconciled. If this is the programme Rousseau undertakes, then the initial terms in which the opposition between the life of man and the life of the citizen is presented are of fundamental importance for understanding the course of the subsequent argument, and so need further consideration here.

The opposition is between the citizen who identifies himself only as a member of a whole, which is his community, and the man who is for himself an individual whole, without reference to others at all. The force of the citizen's identification as member of a larger whole, characterized as the transporting of the individual's 'I', his self-identification, into the collective unity, so that he feels himself to exist only in that unity, is further explained in a statement immediately following the already quoted passage about the citizen. This statement is a description of what Rousseau holds a citizen of the ancient Roman Republic to be like. He says that 'a citizen of Rome was neither Caius, nor Lucius; he was a Roman; and he loved his country exclusively of himself' (p. 9). This quite clearly reveals the way in which the citizen's self-identification excludes his having an individual identity for himself, in the sense of having an identity which distinguishes him from all other men. It is not that he has no identity, for his identity is that of Roman citizen, which distinguishes him from citizens of other cities than Rome, but that this identity is not compatible with his being also for himself a particular differentiated member of the Roman body politic, as Caius or Lucius. His primary identity is a general identity, that of being Roman, which he shares equally with all other Romans, and thus one which does not distinguish him as a particular individual Roman. The man on the other hand is defined in terms of his having an individual identity for himself, which is given independently of his having any relations with others. These two characterizations of man and citizen appear to be opposites, for the one's essence involves the rejection of that individualization which is the essence of the other.

If these two are to be reconciled without altering the essential characterization of either, something peculiar might be supposed to have to happen in the argument. But it is important to note here that the tentativeness with which Rousseau undertakes to reveal this reconciliation reflects an uncertainty in his own mind, that recurs in *Emile* and in the *Social Contract*, as to whether he is able to and has in fact brought about the desired harmony between nature and society, and whether it is not still the case that, to create the good social man or the true citizen, nature has to be suppressed. The subsequent argument will show why this should be so.

The immediate programme of *Emile* is to present an account of an education in accordance with man's nature, the product of which, it is hoped, will be a new kind of man. This education is designed not to fit its product to take up a particular position within a particular society, but to fit him for the status of being a man. 'In leaving my hands,' Rousseau says, 'he will not, I agree, be magistrate, or soldier, or priest; he will be first of all man' (p. 12). In educating Emile for the status of being a man independently of any particular role or set of relations with others that he might come to occupy or possess, the aim is to liberate man from his existing social context. To be educated to take a place in that context is to be educated from the beginning in the false and corrupting ways of that world. In this respect traditional methods and principles of education are useless, for their wisdom appears as senile prejudice, and their usages mere subjection and constraint (p. 13), so that the formation of the new man in requiring an education directed against existing society, necessitates the creation of a new education, embodying a new wisdom and new principles.

THE NEW EDUCATION

Emile, the hero of the story, is handed over at infancy to the care of a tutor, Rousseau, who has sole and total responsibility for his education. The structure of the work is given by the division of Emile's development into five stages: infancy, early childhood, late childhood, adolescence, early manhood. I shall, however, pass over what Rousseau has to say about infancy, for it has little bearing on the main part of the argument, and begin with Emile's childhood, for Rousseau describes the infant as having no sentiment or idea, or even a consciousness of his own existence (p. 58), and it is only with the latter that the life of the individual properly begins. 'The memory,' Rousseau says, 'extends the sense of identity over all the moments of his existence; he becomes truly one, the same and consequently already capable of happiness and misery. It is necessary then to begin to see him at this point as a moral being' (p. 61).

Before developing the general principles of the new education as they apply to childhood, Rousseau begins with some reflexions on the nature of happiness and misery. Every sentiment of pain, he says, is inseparable from the desire of ridding oneself of it, and every idea of pleasure is inseparable from the desire to enjoy it. Desire is common to both, and supposes the privation of that which one desires, which is in itself painful. Hence misery and happiness are defined in terms of the relation between the desires and the capacities to fulfil these desires. It is in the equality or inequality between desire and capacity that misery and happiness consist. Human wisdom can be understood not as involving merely a reduction in the amount of our desires, but a reduction of them in so far as they exceed our capacities, so that what one wills and what one has the power to perform are in exact balance. It is by this means, Rousseau says, that 'all one's capacities being exercised, the soul nevertheless remains at peace with itself, and man is well ordered' (pp. 63–4). This perfect equality between one's powers and one's will was what characterized the condition of natural man of the *Discourse*, and was maintained by the fact that nature had ensured that such faculties of man as reason and imagination, being unnecessary for his existence, were there undeveloped. But so soon as these latent capacities emerge, the equilibrium is destroyed, and it is the imagination that is here said to play the dominant role in its destruction. For the imagination extends for us our idea of what is possible, whether of good or evil, and thus excites and nourishes the desires by offering them the hope of satisfaction. And this does not merely complicate the problem of achieving happiness, but makes happiness unattainable, because the satisfaction of one desire but shows the way to the conception of still more, so that the more satisfaction is obtained, the greater is the dissatisfaction created. Rousseau's recommendation for this situation goes thus:

The real world has its limits; the world of the imagination is infinite; unable to enlarge the former, restrict the latter. (p. 64) and he concludes by apostrophizing man thus:

O man! withdraw your existence into yourself, and you will no longer be miserable ... Your liberty, your power extend no further than your natural capacities; everything else is slavery, illusion, prestige. (p. 68)

The 'everything else' that is slavery, illusion and prestige, is the product of an imagination which makes us exist outside ourselves, either through the desire of what we cannot at present command, or by making us live in the opinions of others, or by forethought of the future, through which we are led to identify ourselves and our happiness with occurrences that take place on the other side of the world. The recommendation to withdraw into ourselves appears as a general recommendation to us to refuse to identify ourselves in relation to persons, goods, future possibilities or states of affairs over which we have no direct control. The aim is the identity of one's power and will, which is taken up again and developed in the following passage.

The only man who carries out his will is the man who, in order to do so, has no need of the arm of another to supplement his own; from which it follows that the first of all goods is not authority, but liberty. The man who is truly free only desires what he is capable of doing and only does what pleases him. That is my fundamental maxim. It is only a matter of applying it to childhood, and all the rules of education will follow. (p. 69)

Rousseau's fundamental maxim is then one of liberty or self-dependence as a condition of happiness, where this means doing in all things one's own will or what pleases one. This looks thoroughly unpromising as a fundamental maxim of an education, since an education is usually taken to involve getting a child to behave and think in ways which it may or may not take easily to, but which can hardly be understood as the natural, unprompted products of the child's own will. As it stands the self-dependence presented to us contains two elements: on the one hand, a practical self-sufficiency, consisting in doing only what one can do by oneself, and on the other the self-sufficiency that consists in not extending one's identity to live outside oneself in relation to goods or persons that one cannot master by oneself. The first, in any literal sense, cannot have application to childhood, since the child is necessarily dependent on the supporting arms of its adults. The liberty or self-dependence of the child must be understood in other terms than these, and while it will not be fully understood until the argument is concluded, we can nevertheless begin to see in what it might consist.

In the above argument about the nature of happiness and misery, it is the imagination which, in causing us to live outside ourselves, destroys the conditions of our happiness by making us dependent on states of affairs subject to the control of others. But one might say the dependence on others, which the child is inevitably subject to, is the product not of imagination but of natural need, so that if an education restricts the child to this natural dependence, by preventing the development of its imagination, it will have preserved the child from acquiring at least certain types of dependencies which are conducive neither to its liberty nor to its happiness. On this account the crucial question is not whether the child is dependent or not, but what sort of dependence the child is to experience. This is clarified in a passage shortly following the above, in which Rousseau makes a distinction between two sorts of dependence, which he not only applies to the problem of education, but immediately says of it that it serves 'to resolve all the contradictions of the social system' (p. 70). He says:

There are two sorts of dependence: dependence on things, which comes from nature; dependence on men, which comes from society. The former, having no moral content, does not interfere with liberty, and engenders no vices: the latter, being disordered, engenders all of them, and it is through it that the master and slave mutually deprave each other. If there is some means of remedying this evil in society, it lies in substituting the law for man, and in arming the general will with a real force, superior to the action of every particular will. If the laws of nations could have, like those of nature, an inflexibility which no human force could ever overcome, dependence on men would become again a dependence on things: we would reunite in a republic all the advantages of the state of nature with those of civil society; one would add to the liberty that maintains man free from vice the morality that raises him to virtue. (pp. 70–1)

How this distinction serves to resolve all the contradictions of the social system will have to be considered later in its due place, but its immediate importance consists in the fact that what Rousseau

44

calls dependence on things is said to be both morally harmless and at the same time held not to affect the subject's liberty. Since in this passage Rousseau conceives of the possibility of a relation between men in society, which takes the form of a dependence on things, it follows that there is held to be a form of human interdependence in society which does not interfere with the individual's liberty. Thus when Rousseau in concluding his present point says, 'to maintain the child in a dependence on things only, you will have followed the order of nature in the progress of his education' (p. 71), this cannot of course mean, turn the child out into physical nature to fend for itself, but rather that there is a way in which the child can be dependent on men, which takes the form of a dependence on things. Whatever this relationship is, and what it is we are to consider, it preserves the liberty of the child, and so is that in terms of which Rousseau's fundamental libertarian maxim is to be understood.

The new education Rousseau proposes, then, has for its fundamental principle liberty, the doing by the child of his own will and not another's. But this of course is not to be interpreted crudely, for this liberty is compatible with, or rather secured by, a dependence of the child on his educator which takes the form of a dependence on things. The child's relation to and dependence on his educator must appear to the child as the same sort of dependent relation that he has to the world of things or physical nature. For Rousseau, this is the only proper way in which to begin the education of a human being, and this method is determined in part by his conception of the child's capacity for understanding human, as distinct from physical, relations. He identifies a radical break in the child's development with the onset of adolescence at the age of fifteen. At that point Rousseau considers it necessary to change his procedure and adopt a different method. The break which comes with adolescence involves a number of changes in the child's experience, but the immediately relevant ground he has for marking the distinction between childhood and adolescence concerns the emergence of reason. There is something that he calls the age of reason, which is not reached until adolescence. But while he initially presents the child as incapable of reasoning, what he turns out to mean is that the child is incapable of reasoning in a theoretical or abstract manner. The child is capable on the other hand of a practical sort of reasoning relevant to his immediate interests and desires. It is, however, the absence in the child of the former capacity which is important for the determination of the child's education. For it is this sort of abstract reason that Rousseau takes to be necessary for the acquisition of a proper and non-corrupt understanding of the distinctively human quality of social relations between men; and believing that the child is incapable of it, he consequently requires that the child should be brought up without acquiring any ideas concerning these relations, but should have present to his consciousness only relations between things (p. 76). It is not that the child, for Rousseau, is by nature incapable of having any comprehension of the human quality of social relations, but rather that the ideas he is capable of having will, unless great care is taken, be false and corrupting ones. If the child is allowed to develop such ideas, and to act in accordance with them, the object of the new education will have been rendered vain from the beginning. It is Rousseau's belief in the natural tendency of the child to be incapable of other than a false understanding that leads to his insistence that every effort should be made to keep the child ignorant until adolescence of all moral and social matters, and to present to his consciousness only relations between things. Every effort should be made, but Rousseau is not confident that it will be possible to avoid teaching the child something of these adult matters; if it becomes inevitable, the instruction should nevertheless be minimal and in a manner to be specified.

In respect of the child, then, the content and manner of education are to be determined by the requirement that the child's relation to his educator should be an induction in physical and not moral nature. It is what is involved in this conception of the proper relationship between child and educator that constitutes the fundamental revolutionary element in Rousseau's educational thought, and it is on this that I shall concentrate.

What is involved can be most clearly grasped in the first instance in terms of the form of control that the educator is to exercise over the child. This is because Rousseau conceives of the education of the child as largely a negative one, ensuring that the child does not acquire bad habits and corrupt conceptions. Nevertheless, the child cannot be left to himself without some control being exercised over his behaviour. Rousseau begins by distinguishing the form of control he recommends from on the one hand the indulgence that produces a spoilt child, and on the other the discipline that reduces the child to a cowed condition. What Rousseau offers is, however, not a mean between the two, but something altogether different. An early statement as to how the child should be related to others goes thus:

Keep away from them [children] with the greatest care servants who provoke, irritate or render them impatient: they are a hundred times more dangerous than the injuries of the air or of the seasons. So long as children only find resistance in things and never in wills, they will become neither fractious nor bad-tempered, and will conserve themselves in better health. (p. 47)

Although this passage seems to require no human opposition to the child's will at all, but that the child should literally be allowed to do what he wills, this is not what Rousseau means, nor could mean, and in the following passage something more is evidently envisaged: 'Only oppose to his injudicious desires physical obstacles or punishments which arise out of the actions themselves, and which he will recall on the relevant occasions; without forbidding him to do wrong, it is sufficient to prevent him' (p. 71). Clearly human opposition to the child's will is to occur when necessary, but it appears that it should take place without allowing the child to see and feel that it is in fact a human will that is opposing his own. The controlling human will should work through opposing things to the child's will and not through the direct imposition of will on the child. It seems that it is for this reason that punishment of the child should not appear as punishment, that is to say in its traditional form, for in that form punishment is present to the child directly as a human will antagonistic to his own and imposed in an unpleasant way on him. Punishment, Rousseau says later, should not appear to children as punishment, but 'as the natural consequences of their bad action' (p. 94). In the latter form the unpleasant content of punishment will appear to the child as a natural and inevitable law consequent upon his acting in a certain way and having nothing to do with human, i.e. non-natural, contrivances or requirements.

The above account implies that the child is not to see himself as dependent upon or controlled by his human educator at all, but literally only on things. The human educator would seem to be required to exist in the background as a controlling power that is not seen to control at all. But in the following passage the emphasis is altered:

Never command him to do anything, whatever it is in the world: absolutely nothing. Do not even allow him to imagine that you pretend to have any authority over him. Let him know only that he is weak and you are strong; that through his condition and yours, he is necessarily at your mercy; let him know this, learn it, feel it; let him feel on his proud head from early on the hard yoke that nature imposes on man, the heavy yoke of necessity, under which every finite being must bow; let him see this necessity in things and never in the caprice of men; let the bridle which restrains him be force and not authority. (p. 79)

In this passage, the control of the human educator is to appear directly to the child, but only so long as it takes the form of superior force and not authority. In view of what has immediately gone before, it might be supposed that the value of force as opposed to authority here consists in the possibility of exercising the former so that it will appear to the child like a natural force, having no element of a human will opposed to and impinging on the child's own, whereas authority necessarily involves the appearance of such a human will, for it openly requires the child to conform his will to the will claiming authority. But it would be very odd if the child were not to see something like will implicit in the force exercised against him, and indeed in the continuation of the above passage will is allowed to make its appearance:

When he must abstain from doing something, do not forbid him; prevent him from doing it without explanations or reasonings; what you are prepared to grant him, grant at his first word, without solicitations, prayers, above all without conditions. Grant with pleasure, refuse only with repugnance, but let your refusals be irrevocable; let no importuning weaken you; let the NO once pronounced be a wall of bronze against which the child will not have exhausted his forces five or six times without attempting further to upset it. (pp. 79–80)

In this case the child must be able to see that the being on which he depends for the satisfaction of some of his desires has a power,

separately identifiable from that being's superior strength, to determine whether his desires will be satisfied or not. The idea would
seem to be that this power must appear to the child to be quite inflexible once determined in a certain way, so that he must submit
to its determination as to something which he has no means of
influencing or controlling. But if this is Rousseau's idea, the point
he would now seem to be making is not that the child should not see
himself as opposed by and having to submit to a human power that
is quite different from anything he could experience in the world
of things, but that this power when exercised against the child should
be inflexible. However, if the point is the inflexible use of this human
power, why should Rousseau specifically exclude the exercise of
authority as a means of controlling the child? For cannot authority
be exercised inflexibly also? The distinction between Rousseau's
mode of control and the authoritative mode must lie elsewhere.
Authority proceeds by way of commands, orders, requests to the
child to do or not to do something, which thus require on the
part of the child some positive action, whether it is doing or desist-
ing from doing. The child has explicitly to conform his will to the
will demanding obedience. But in Rousseau's example of the exercise of will against the child, this is not necessarily so. No positive
action of the child is required, but only the acceptance of what this
power has determined. No explicit conforming of the child's will in
action to the will of another is involved, but merely the yielding
to the fate that has been determined for him.

What Rousseau appears to have in mind, then, is that the control
exercised by educator over child, whether through superior force
or will, should not be experienced by the child as requiring the
explicit conformity of his own will in action to the will of another.
One reason for this appears in the following passage:

In any case there is here no mean: one must either demand nothing, or
bend him to the most perfect obedience. The worst education is to leave
him fluctuating between his will and yours, and to dispute unceasingly,
which of you will be the master; I would prefer a hundred times more that
he should be master always. (p. 80)

Authority in requiring positive action on the part of the child always
leaves the child with the choice of acting or not acting in compliance

with the order, and so carries with it the difficulty of obtaining the required action on the part of the child without a perpetually recurring conflict. On the other hand in Rousseau's method this difficulty is removed, since no orders are given, and the only choice open to the child is between a quiet submission and the creation of a disturbance, which can be ignored or prevented. The perfect obedience that Rousseau's method is designed to produce is not of course supposed to be obedience, but rather submission for as he says, 'the words of obedience and command will be proscribed from his vocabulary, even more those of duty and obligation; but those of force, necessity, weakness and constraint should hold a large place in it' (p. 76). The submission is to a greatly superior will-power, which if necessary can be backed by force, and this submission is acceptable for Rousseau in a way in which obedience to an authoritative will is not. One reason why this should be so is, as already indicated, that the exclusion of the authoritative mode of control removes or greatly reduces the possibility of conflicts of will. But this does not seem a very satisfactory reason, since it is not clear that the effective use of authority cannot achieve the same result, namely the perfect submission to the will claiming authority. What is clear is that authority is to be excluded and that what is to be substituted for it is to be described as the submission of the child to the necessity of things.

In the case Rousseau gives of the exercise of will to control the child, it is only a matter of refusing or granting something to the child, and no action is required of him. But if authority is to be excluded altogether, no action can ever be explicitly required of the child. If the educator is to bring about behaviour of a desired sort in the child, this must be secured in another way. As before what this involves in general terms is rendering the child 'docile and compliant by the force of things alone' (p. 80), and not through verbal lessons, authoritative requests, commands, orders and so forth. How we are to understand this can be seen from a consideration of the story that Rousseau tells of his relations with a child whom he had been asked to look after during the absence of the child's tutor (pp. 122–7). This child had through early pampering become a little tyrant, and expected his every whim to be attended to by adults. Rousseau describes two incidents in which the child attempts to reduce Rousseau to the position of his slave, and how, in defeating these attempts, Rousseau succeeds in bending the child's will to his own. In the first incident the child rises in the middle of the night and demands Rousseau's attention. Rousseau begins complaisantly, but as the disturbances continue, and the child's intentions become obvious, Rousseau finally ignores him. As a result the child becomes furious and pretends to destroy the room. Rousseau finally unable to maintain his original policy of completely ignoring the child, loses his temper, takes the child into a neighbouring room where there is little for the child to damage, and locks him in. The child's fury redoubles, but receiving no attention and worn out by his exertions, he falls asleep. In the second incident everything is planned by Rousseau: Rousseau proposes to the child to go for a walk, but the child, interested in what he is doing, refuses. Later, becoming bored with his activities, the child demands of Rousseau to be taken for the walk he had at first refused, but Rousseau, asserting that *he* is interested in what he is doing, declines to take him. The child, angry at having his will frustrated, threatens to go by himself, but Rousseau takes no notice and the child tries to get a servant to accompany him. The servant, however, has been instructed by Rousseau to say that he too is busy, so that the child is forced to carry out his threat to go alone. Once alone in the streets the child becomes the object of derogatory public comment and mockery, but to ensure that the child comes to no harm, Rousseau has arranged for a friend, unknown to the child, to watch over him and bring him home when he becomes frightened and distraught. Thus the child is eventually returned confused and humiliated, and Rousseau receives him 'without reproaches and without mockery, but with some gravity' (p. 126). Commenting on these episodes Rousseau says:

It was by these and other similar means that during the short time I was with him, I succeeded in getting him to do all that I wished, without prescribing or forbidding him anything, without sermons or exhortations, and without boring him with useless lessons. Also so long as I was speaking, he was content; but my silence made him afraid; he understood that something was not going well, and the lesson always came from the thing itself. (pp. 126–7)

Although this is an extreme case of a spoilt child requiring extreme measures, the story nevertheless illustrates Rousseau's principles effectively enough. The child is brought to the required state of perfect obedience neither by the direct confrontation of wills, through either authoritative instructions or reprimands, nor even by simple orders backed by threats, but by exposing the inability of the child to fend for himself, and thus his necessary dependence on and submission to Rousseau. The weakness of the child and the strength of the adult is brought home to the child by the adult's refusal to cooperate. In this way the child is said to learn his lesson of submission, *from the thing itself*, and not from Rousseau, by which Rousseau must mean that the child learns from the experience of his own unavoidable incapacity the necessity of submitting.

In this story the child submits, but not by openly conforming his will to Rousseau's will and so obeying Rousseau, for, as Rousseau openly demands nothing of the child, this is impossible. In so far as the child submits because he feels that he cannot do without Rousseau's support, he is said to be submitting to the necessity of things, and the idea would seem to be that in yielding to what he feels as necessary, the liberty of the child's will is not infringed. Furthermore this sort of dependence is held by Rousseau to be orderly as contrasted with the disorderly nature of the dependence that involves open submission to another will. In this respect the child's submission to his educator is similar to the submission of one natural man to another that Rousseau supposed would occur from time to time in a state of nature. For in such a state any conflict between the desires of one man and the desires of another was seen to be resolved simply by the superior force of the stronger; the difference between the latter submission and the child's being that in the state of nature the inferior goes off to satisfy his desires elsewhere, while the child must remain in a continuous state of dependent inferiority. But just as in the state of nature one man in submitting temporarily to another is submitting to the morally harmless necessity of things, i.e. the unavoidable natural superiority of the other; so the child, in submitting to the adult in the way Rousseau requires, is submitting to the necessity of nature, and he learns his lesson from things, i.e. from the nature of his unavoidable weakness, and not from authoritative pronouncements. In neither case does submission take the form of explicit control by another will, to which the inferior has to conform his will, so that in neither case does it appear that the liberty of the will of the inferior is infringed, for neither has explicitly to learn to do the will of another. In the case of the child, however, we would have to say that no control of the child's will is *openly* exercised, because control of the child's will by Rousseau's will is indeed what is secured, albeit indirectly. Why the authoritative method of control must be excluded, then, is because it aims at such open control of the child's will. It is in the absence of such open control that Rousseau's libertarian principle consists, so that the child is supposed to be doing his own will when his submission is brought about by indirect means.

But as so far presented the method appears as a negative means of control, a means of preventing the child from doing certain things and of securing a sufficient docility and compliance in his behaviour. It is not clearly adequate for teaching the child standards or principles of good behaviour towards others. In this respect, however, it is in conformity with Rousseau's belief that the child should, if possible, know nothing about human relations until the age of reason, and Rousseau, as we have also seen, represents it as a negative education designed, not to teach the child anything, so much as to prevent the child from acquiring the habits of vice and the spirit of error (p. 83). To proceed thus negatively at this stage is what Rousseau takes to be desirable. Nevertheless, he recognizes that it may be necessary with some 'naturally violent' children to introduce them to an understanding of human relations and the behaviour required towards others, which with gentler and more tranquil children can be left until adolescence (p. 88). The introduction of children to the idea of what is good and what is not good behaviour towards others immediately raises the problem of authority in acute form. For in so far as one presents what is required as standards of right behaviour, which exist independently of the child's will, as arrangements governing the adult world, and to which the child is required to conform his will, the previous good work will have been destroyed and the liberty of the child's will infringed. To avoid authority reasserting its claims and in order to maintain undiminished the libertarian principle, Rousseau proposes that what the child is to learn in these matters, he must learn from his own experience and relate to his own immediate interest while the behaviour produced he must be able to see as the product of his own self-determination.

What this involves can be seen from a consideration of two incidents Rousseau introduces. In the first he proposes to introduce his child, Emile, to the existence of property rights and to a respect for them (pp. 89–92). Rousseau interests Emile in gardening and arranges for Emile to cultivate a small garden plot which has already been sown by the gardener. Emile takes a great interest in the progress of his plants, and is encouraged by Rousseau to believe that he has a property in the plants and the land. However, one day he finds that the gardener has uprooted them in anger at the destruction of his own work. Subsequently an agreement is made by which Emile is to have a part of the garden for his own use. From this incident Emile is supposed to understand and respect the right of property as consisting in the right of the first occupant by labour. Now although Rousseau believes that this is the only real foundation for property rights, it is of course a totally misleading account of the actual property rights that existed in either his or our own time, but the advantage of this account of them from Rousseau's immediate point of view is that it presents these rights as arising out of individual effort which owed nothing to others and which Emile can achieve for himself. Emile can see his rights and the rights of others as arising out of each person's own will and effort, and so as what each creates by and for himself without relation to or dependence on others. He does not have to recognize the actual rights of others for what they are, namely as existing only through arrangements made independently of his will, and to which his will is authoritatively required to conform. In this way a sense of property rights is given to the child without recourse to the claims of authority.

In the second incident we have a child who breaks things, especially windows (pp. 92–3). As he goes on breaking the windows that are replaced, the child is not reproved and is punished only by being removed to a room without windows and locked in. He is made to feel the misery of his position, until it is suggested, not by his educator, but a servant or someone else that he make an agreement with his educator by which he is given his liberty in return for an engagement on his part not to break any more windows. The point here is that the behaviour which the child undertakes should be the result of a convention which the child can see as the product of his own will. This is generalized by Rousseau thus:

> If his difficult nature compels me to make some convention with him, I will so well arrange my measures that the proposition always comes from him and never from me; that, when he has engaged himself, he should always have an immediate and felt interest in fulfilling his engagement; and that should he ever fail in it, his lie should bring down on him evils that he sees as arising out of the order of things, and not the vengeance of his tutor. (p. 96)

Thus when it is necessary to teach the child to respect persons or a person's things, that is for the child to acquire an understanding of right behaviour, Rousseau's principle demands that this behaviour be not presented as required by adult standards and endorsed by the educator's authority, but as the product of conventions, agreements and so on and so appear to the child as coming from himself and good for himself, as that in which he has an immediate interest. In this way the desired behaviour is brought about without affecting the child's self-mastery, for he and not others is responsible for the behaviour.

It will now be obvious what method is to be applied in the education of the child's mind, or in the imparting of knowledge to the child. This teaching is hardly to occur before the age of twelve, when according to Rousseau there is a short period before the onset of adolescence at the age of fifteen, when the child is particularly suited to mental effort of the required kind. The method is well known, as governing all progressive education, and follows directly on from the previous account, so that it need only be briefly considered. In the first place the acquisition of knowledge by the child should be determined by reference to the child's immediate interest (p. 116), and should consist of matter which enables the child to extend his power over the world, that is to say his control of natural forces. It should be a utilitarian education in the sense of being directed at what is immediately useful to the child, and not a bookish one. What the child learns, he should not learn from his educator, but should discover from his own experience, from the world and from facts. He is to teach his educator rather than be taught by him (p. 157). He is not to learn science but invent it for himself (p. 186). And although Rousseau of course recognizes that this involves guidance and prompting, suggesting to the child problems and questions and ensuring that he finds the right answers, such guidance should be as little as possible and should not appear to the child (p. 191). The child should appear to be doing it all himself.

What lies behind this insistence on the child's self-education is the fear of authority. Thus: 'Compelled to learn from himself, he uses his own reason and not the reason of others; for in order to allow nothing to opinion, one must grant nothing to authority' (p. 242). Or this: 'If you once substitute in his mind authority for reason, he will reason no more; he will be no more than the plaything of the opinion of others' (p. 186). Authority in this sphere, however, cannot be represented directly as requiring the child's will to conform to another will, for it is a matter of the child's understanding and not his will. But the consequences of teaching in the authoritative mode are nevertheless as serious from Rousseau's point of view, for as the above quotations point out the subjection of the child to intellectual authority involves the use by the child of the reason of others, even if the child then appropriates that reason for himself. The child learns to attend to and so become dependent on his educator's reason and not on his own reason alone. And behind this lies opinion: the child will, even if not slavishly follow, at least become responsive to, the opinions and judgements of others, and in doing so will have lost an essential element of his self-dependence and self-mastery. This method of developing the child's mind is presented by Rousseau as superior to the old authoritative mode from the point of view simply of the child's acquisition of knowledge. The child will not so much know more than a child brought up under the old régime, but will be much better off in respect of his capacity to build on the knowledge he already possesses. For the new method teaches him how to acquire knowledge and gives him an interest in so doing, whereas the old did neither, for its essence was to dictate. But whether this is so or not, it is quite clear that the invention of this method and its recommendation springs not from a concern to improve the efficiency of teaching, but from the moral impetus provided by Rousseau's conception of the proper relationship that should exist between educator and child. For it is Rousseau's belief that it is never as important for the child to learn as it is that he do nothing against his will (p. 192).

We have seen that there is both in the negative and positive aspects of Rousseau's educational programme one consistent principle, which at all times dictates the methods to be pursued: the libertarian principle that the child should do in all things his own will and not another's. But this is to be understood as the requirement that the child should never have to accept openly the will or authority of his educator. In so far as the educator is in fact controlling the child's will, bringing about certain behaviour, or guiding his thoughts, this should never appear to the child, but on the contrary the child should always be able to feel that what he does is the product of his own determination alone, whether this is in submitting to a dependence on his educator, recognizing the claims of others or acquiring knowledge. There is, then, involved in this programme a certain duplicity practised on the child, for what is always important is not so much the reality of the child's self-determination, but the appearance of this to the child. This is quite obvious in the case of the refractory child discussed above. The child's submission is brought about by the exploitation of the child's inability to fend for himself in a public world. It is indeed true that this submission is different from the child's conforming his will openly to an authoritative will; nevertheless the submission comes about through the collapse of the child's will, and the surrendering of it to Rousseau's, so that the reality is the control of the child's will by Rousseau's. Only this reality preserves the appearance of the child's liberty in so far as it appears as the result, not of anything explicitly demanded of the child, but of his own self-determination. The refractory child is an extreme case, but Rousseau describes this child as being brought to a state of docile compliance, and docile compliance is what Rousseau seems to think will be the natural condition of a child educated according to his method. But a condition of compliance is one in which the child's will is, as with the refractory child, effectively dominated by a superior whatever the appearance may be. Furthermore in the case of the child's learning right behaviour through conventions and in his acquisition of knowledge the reality is also different from the appearance. What is supposed to be the case for the child is that he proposes the agreement to suit his own interests, but the reality is that the educator controls both the conditions which determine what is in the child's interests and the terms of the agreement, while in respect of acquiring knowledge the appearance is of the child using his own reason alone, and the obvious reality that he must in one way or another use the reason of his educator in order to develop his own.

In case we should have missed the way in which Rousseau's method is concerned with the appearance rather more than with the reality of the child's self-determination Rousseau emphasizes it for us. Thus in again rejecting the traditional attempt of the educator to impose his authority on the child, Rousseau says this:

Adopt an opposite method with your pupil: let him always believe himself to be the master, but let it be you who is. *There is no subjection so perfect as one which preserves the appearance of liberty; in this way one captures the will itself.* The poor child who knows nothing and can do nothing, is he not at your mercy? Do you not dispose in relation to him of his whole environment? Are you not able to affect him as you please? His labours, his games, his pleasures and his pains, is not everything in your hands without his knowing it? Of course he should only do what he wants to do, but he should only want what you wish him to do; he should not take a step without your foreknowledge; he should not open his mouth without your knowing what he will say. (p. 121; my emphasis)

If the child's will is not really free, but the child only possesses for himself the appearance of freedom, in appearing to be master, and is thus all the more effectively controlled, because manipulated from behind without his awareness, what then is the point of Rousseau's whole programme? Is it a matter of indifference from the point of view of the programme's aim, whether the child possesses the reality or only the appearance of freedom? We cannot answer this question by reference to the declared fundamental principle of the programme, for this is the principle of liberty itself, which cannot therefore tell us why Rousseau should seem to be content with its appearance only. If we are going to understand why Rousseau should not be worried by the gap which opens up between the appearance and reality of freedom, we must discover a point to the enterprise which lies beyond the libertarian principle.

It is not the case that this educational programme has no reference beyond itself, for it is put forward in the wider context of Rousseau's thought about the social problem. It exists as a preliminary part of a more general programme, which was seen to be aimed at overcoming the contradictions and corruption that had entered man's life with his socialization by bringing about a reconciliation between nature and society. So, if we are to find a point to the libertarian principle beyond itself, which explains the curious duplicity involved in its application, it is likely to consist in the way in which the principle and its application support the general aims of Rousseau's programme. The social problem, as it was conceived in the *Discourse*, con-sisted in the transformation of man's self-love from its natural form as *amour de soi* into *amour-propre*, which went together with the emergence of a new consciousness in man, by which he comes to live for others, and not as in nature for himself alone. And while of course the social problem has got to be resolved in such a way that man can come in some new and uncorrupting way to live for others, nevertheless the initial problem arises out of the social fact of this corrupt form of living for others. This is what in the first instance has to be avoided, and seeing the libertarian principle of the new education in this wider context will help us to understand what the point of it is.

In respect of the early negative aspect of this education in which the child is not to be taught anything, but merely prevented from acquiring bad habits, Rousseau puts forward as an indisputable maxim that the first movements of nature are always right, and that there is no original perversity in the human heart. And he goes on to say:

The only passion natural to man is *amour de soi-même*, or *amour-propre* understood in an extended sense. This *amour-propre* in or relative to one-self is good and useful; and as it involves no necessary relation to others, it is in this respect naturally indifferent; it only becomes good or bad through the application that is made of it and the relations one gives it.

59

Until the guide of *amour-propre*, which is reason, can develop, it is there-fore necessary that a child should do nothing because it is seen or heard, nothing in a word by relation to others, but only what nature demands of him; and then he will do nothing but good. (p. 81)

In this passage the distinction hitherto maintained between the two forms of self-love, *amour de soi* and *amour-propre*, appears super-ficially to be confused, but only because Rousseau is now distinguish-ing two forms of *amour-propre*, which exactly correspond to the old *amour de soi* and *amour-propre*. The *amour-propre* which is identical with the old *amour de soi* is the love of self in or relative to oneself, and thus without relation to others. It is this passion which is still maintained as the original natural passion, and according to which, until a certain stage, which is adolescence, when the child's reason has developed sufficiently to act as controlling guide of the other *amour-propre*, the child must be left to act. For the child to act in accordance with this passion only, it is necessary that the child do nothing by reference to his relations with others, do nothing because he is seen or heard by others, which is to say that the child must never be affected in his actions by the fact that he is observed, judged or watched over by others. In so far as this aim is realized the consciousness of the child would be identical with the original consciousness of natural man, whose concern was solely for how he was for himself, and not how he was in relation to others. But while it made some sense to suppose natural man living for himself alone without attending to his relations with others, because in no way did he depend on others, the child's necessary and thoroughgoing dependence on his educator would seem to make it impossible for the child to possess a similar consciousness. The child in submitting to his educator must surely act by reference to his relations with him. But here the point of the submission and dependence that Rousseau's method brings about is that the child submits for his own good, by reference to what he needs for himself, and not by reference to what others want of him. His reference in his actions remains him-self and not others.

Rousseau's idea is that this form of self-love is in itself morally harmless, so that if the child acts always in accordance with it, he will do nothing but good; not of course morally good things, but naturally good things. So the aim is to preserve this natural goodness and innocence in the child by preventing him from acquiring the consciousness through which he considers himself in his relations with others. To do this it is necessary to make the child's 'well-being independent both of the wills and judgements of others' (p. 96), so that the child does not come to identify his well-being as dependent on how he exists for others. Thus Rousseau says of his Emile immediately prior to his adolescence: 'He considers himself without relation to others, and is content that others do not think of him. He demands nothing of anybody and believes he owes nothing to anybody. He is alone in human society' (p. 244). Of course understood as requiring that relations with others should have no meaning or value for the child, that the child should be without affection and without support, this statement is a monstrous absurdity. Rousseau's point must be that although the child possesses the affection and support of his educator, this does not make the child live by reference to this relation. And for this to be the case the child would have to see the relationship as a one-way relationship, in which the attentions of the other serve his needs, and for which nothing on his part is required. For as Rousseau says:

A child is naturally inclined towards benevolence, because he sees that everyone who approaches him is concerned to help him, and because he derives from this observation the habit of a favourable sentiment towards his species; but in so far as he extends his relations, his needs and dependence, whether active or passive, the sentiment of his relations to others awakes, and produces that of duties and preferences. Thus the child becomes imperious, jealous, deceitful and vindictive. If one forces him to obey, not seeing the utility of what is commanded, he attributes it to caprice, to the intention to torment him, and he mutinies. If one obeys him, as soon as he meets any resistance, he sees it as a rebellion, as an intention to resist him; he beats the chair or the table for having disobeyed. *Amour de soi*, which is concerned only with ourselves, is content when our true needs are satisfied; but *amour-propre*, which involves comparisons with others, is never content and would not know how to be, because this sentiment in preferring ourselves to others, demands also that others prefer us to themselves; which is impossible. (pp. 248–9)

In restricting the child to the sole passion of *amour de soi*, by which the child refers everything to himself, the child will of course be preserved from the passion of *amour-propre*, which is the point of entry of vices and corruption. Not that this *amour-propre* will never make its appearance, for as we shall see it very soon does, but that it must not be allowed to appear before the child's reason is in a position to direct it into desirable channels.

We are now in a position to see why Rousseau should be content with the appearance and not the reality of the child's freedom. The libertarian principle and the method it requires is not put forward for its own sake, but is aimed at preventing the child from identifying his well-being by reference to his relations with others, and so preventing the child from coming to exist for himself in these relations and not for himself alone. How this is achieved can be grasped in the first place negatively by considering how the traditional authoritative mode of education prevents this objective from being realized. Authority proceeds through the requirement that the child explicitly conform his will and behaviour to the will of another. In so far as this authority is reasonably effective in bringing about the required conformity, and the behaviour is not secured by terrorizing the child, it can only be because the child implicitly recognizes his well-being as dependent on the relationship he has with the person in authority. The child agrees to do the will of another because he sees himself as having an existence for the author of this will, and desires that this existence be pleasing to the other. To feel this it is necessary that the child feel also that the person in authority exists for him, so that a mutual relationship being created, in which each exists for the other, the child can possess a sufficient confidence in his existence for the other, to allow him to conform his will and behaviour when this is required. But it is only because the child comes to see himself in terms of his existence for the person in authority, that authority can exist at all. Were this not the case, and leaving aside Rousseau's method, the only alternative way of securing conformity would be by terrorizing the child, so that the child submits out of fear for himself. But this would not be authority. The successful exercise of authority, then, involves just those conditions which Rousseau thinks must at all costs be avoided. It presupposes in the child the desire for an existence for others, which generates *amour-propre* and the vicious passions, at a time when according to Rousseau, he is not in a position to do other than succumb to them.

Rousseau's method is opposed to authority because its aim is to prevent the emergence in the child of the sort of consciousness that is the necessary condition of authority. The aim is to ensure that the reference of the child's self-concern is never outside himself to his existence for others, and thus that the only person he is concerned to exist for and so please is himself. The details of Rousseau's method all follow from this requirement. In the first place the attentions that the child receives from others must be seen by the child as attentions to what he needs for himself, in which indeed he shows pleasure and gratification, but for which no positive response to his benefactors is required. In the second place the child's submission to a necessary dependence on his educator must be done without any concern on the child's part to exist well for his educator. The dependence must be seen as a necessary means to obtain what the child wants for himself. The educator exists as a means to the child's self-satisfaction, where this self-satisfaction is defined independently of the relation to the educator. Thirdly, where the child is related to others through contracts, bargains and agreements, although the child has to do something for others in order to obtain his part of the bargain, what he does to satisfy others can be seen by the child purely as a means to obtain what he wants for himself. The child's ultimate point of reference is his own interest defined independently of a relation to others. Fourthly, in so far as in respect of the child's mental development the child is allowed to believe that he is using his own reason always and never the reason of another, he does not have to be aware of referring his thoughts and ideas to another mind and observe how that other mind considers them. He can think of himself as mentally existing by and for himself, without relation to other minds. In this way the child is to exist, like natural man, for himself alone, for his well-being for himself is not defined in terms of his relations to others, but independently of such relations. Others exist for him only as means to his independently defined self-satisfaction. The child is to be alone in human society in the sense that, as persons for whom he might wish to exist, others have no meaning for him.

Rousseau believes that for the child always to act by reference to his well-being conceived independently of relations to others, the child must do his own will and never another's. And as we have seen it is likely to be the case that this independence will be broken down if the child is explicitly required to obey an authority. But all that is strictly necessary is that the child see himself as doing his own will, so that the appearance of the child's freedom is sufficient to bring about the desired result. There is, however, here no alternative, for the educator must watch over and control the child, as Rousseau makes clear, and this can only be done, while achieving the desired object, by determining unbeknown to the child how the child shall exercise his will. The child in fact does the will of his educator without awareness that this is what he is doing.

The above suggests that the child is not to see himself as in any way dependent on his educator, but that this dependence is concealed through the educator's remaining in the background only, arranging matters according to his idea of what the child should do without letting this appear to the child. This is, however, not only implausible, but not what Rousseau says. Rousseau's child is to accept a necessary dependence on his educator. This explicit dependence is to be compatible both with the independence of the child's well-being and with the child's doing his own will and not his educator's. This will be secured so long as the child accepts the dependence as a necessary means of obtaining what he wants for himself. The freedom of the child's will is preserved in so far as the child sees the educator's support and services as things which he needs to achieve his own satisfaction. The freedom arises from the independence of the child's ends, his independently defined well-being, together with the instrumentality for the child of his dependence on his educator. The dependence is merely a means of achieving his will and not an infringement of it. Only if the dependence on the educator is itself seen as constitutive of his well-being will this affect the independence of the child's will. For then what the child wills cannot be determined apart from the will of his educator, and the independence of his will is lost together with the independence of his well-being. This latter relation would be for Rousseau a dependence on men as men, which is disorderly, whereas if the child's dependence on his educator is for the child instrumental to his well-being, the dependence will be as on things, which is how Rousseau conceives of the proper relation.

Rousseau's account of the proper relation between child and educator as one in which the child sees his dependence as a dependence on things could serve very well as a description of the response of a radically disturbed child, who, having lost all confidence in those adults in relation to whom he conceived himself as existing, withdraws into himself, and refuses to consider others except as things from which benefits may or may not be secured, but which are not persons to whom he can commit his existence. The relation between child and educator in Rousseau appears as one in which each treats the other as a thing to be manipulated, and not as a human relationship in which each exists for the other by conceiving of his well-being in terms of the relationship. While it would seem not impossible to achieve this object, we can see from parts of Rousseau's account of his method that things are not likely to go so far. For example, if we consider again the way in which Rousseau reduces the refractory child to a docile compliance, we can see that, although Rousseau claims that the child learns his lesson from things, this is not the case. The child quite obviously requires not the physical but the emotional support of Rousseau, which, when denied the child in his hour of need, brings about a collapse of the child's independence and a submission to Rousseau's will. The child subsequently becomes so dependent on Rousseau that he learns from Rousseau's silences that 'something was not going well' (see above, p. 51). Rousseau says of this that the lesson came from the thing itself, but it is obvious that what the child perceives in Rousseau's silences is Rousseau's disapproval, and if this is to mean anything to the child so as to affect his behaviour, it can only be because the child has come to identify his well-being in terms of how he exists for Rousseau. He does not treat the relation to Rousseau as instrumental to but as constitutive of his well-being, and does not see Rousseau as a thing, but as a person for whom he desires to exist. But in so far as this desire of the child to exist for Rousseau receives no explicit satisfaction in Rousseau's open approval or indeed disapproval, but only implicitly between the lines and in the silences, the pretence can be maintained that the child is dependent only on things. The consequence of this procedure will not, however, be the independence of the child's will, but an almost total dependence. For by never giving the child a secure confidence in his existence for the other, but nevertheless maintaining the child in a need for it, the child will be deprived of the ability to achieve even that degree of independence that he is capable of.

Whatever the practice of the new method is likely to involve, its fundamental idea is that of preserving the presumed natural egoism of the child by ensuring that the child conceives of his well-being independently of his relations with other people. That the result will not be a human relationship should not disturb Rousseau, since he believes that the child should not be introduced to human relations, and so come to understand men as persons rather than as things, until the child has changed into an adolescent and arrived at the age of reason. Rousseau, of course, supposes that this method will secure the happiness of the child. But this could only be the case if the child had naturally no need of an existence for the persons on whom he is dependent, but could, like natural man, be sufficient for himself. This seems unlikely, and in so far as it is false, Rousseau's whole conception of the right education for a child would be a monstrous absurdity. However, Rousseau's method of education is not designed simply to procure the maximum happiness for the child but also to prepare the ground for the new way in which men are to be related to each other in society. The significance of the new education cannot therefore be fully grasped until the content of the new social consciousness is itself understood; nevertheless we can acquire a proximate understanding by considering what it is designed to exclude.

In the first place the negative aim of the education is, as we have seen, to prevent the well-being of the child becoming dependent on how he exists for others. The reason for this is that with such dependence the reference of the child's well-being and actions will not be back to himself but outside himself to the opinions and judgements of others. This sort of living outside oneself was, as we saw in the *Discourse*, the identifying characteristic of the corrupt consciousness. If the purpose of Rousseau's enquiry is to discover the terms in which an alternative to this corrupt consciousness can be conceived, and to show what sort of education such an alternative requires, then it is clear that to allow the child to live in the consciousness of others is to allow the child to acquire the corrupt consciousness as the foundation of his social being. The child will have been captured for the old corrupt world, for he will have had a long experience in living in the presence of others before any possibility exists of bringing about his reformation. When the possibility first arises with adolescence, the child will already be at home in a particular human world and have a solid identity for himself defined in terms of his relation to and existence for that world, so that the idea of the reformed society will have no attractions for him. For these attractions to carry their full weight, the child must have arrived at adolescence unattached to others and alone in human society. He will then be ready and receptive for the transformation that will make of him a new man and a new moral being.

MORALITY

Emile, brought up according to the new principles, must be supposed to be at the onset of adolescence still living for himself alone, governed by the sole passion of *amour de soi* and ignorant of all understanding of human relations. With adolescence this ignorance is to be broken down.

The study appropriate to man is that of his relationships. So long as he knows himself only through his physical being, he should study himself through his relations to things: this is the employment of his childhood; when he begins to sense his moral being, he should study himself through his relations with men; this is the employment of his whole life, to begin at the point which we have now reached. (p. 249)

That this study should begin at this point and neither earlier nor later is because the point we have arrived at is that of the adolescent's emerging sexuality.[1] As soon as he experiences through this desire the need for another, he ceases to be an isolated being, living

[1] This does not contradict what was said on pp. 45–6 above about reason. The point is that with emerging sexuality Emile's introduction to others can no longer be postponed. But at the same time an awareness of others will now not necessarily be harmful, since his reason can be developed to counter the dangers this awareness brings.

for himself alone, and becomes ready to establish relations with his species. What the adolescent experiences in this desire is not, however, simply the natural instinct of sex, for the movement of nature is merely the attraction of one sex to the other, a movement which makes no distinction between one woman and another, the first always being the best. The adolescent's instinct is modified by choice, preference and personal attachment, which are not given in nature, but are the product, Rousseau says, of enlightenment, prejudice and habit (p. 249). His natural desire, that is to say, is experienced in a socialized form, the result of which is that with *amour-passion amour-propre* arrives on the scene.

The preference which one accords, one wishes to obtain; love must be reciprocal. To be loved, one must make oneself desirable; to be preferred, one must make oneself more desirable than another, more desirable than every other, at least in the eyes of the beloved. Hence the first observations of one's fellow men; hence the first comparisons of oneself with them, and so emulation, rivalry and jealousy. (p. 250)

Since the adolescent's consciousness at this stage is not supposed to be social at all, but natural in its purest form, aware only of things and not of men, one may wonder why his sexual desire should immediately manifest itself in a social form, rather than as natural indiscriminate lust. Sexual desire is supposed to explain the emergence in the adolescent of a social interest in others, but since sexual desire does not naturally produce this interest, but only a socialized sexual desire, the origin of the social interest remains unexplained. But this implausibility derives from the implausibility of Rousseau's supposition that the child arrived at adolescence will have no awareness of human relations, and so will not already be a social, rather than a natural, being. Such an awareness the adolescent will of course possess, and it is because he will already be a social being, that his emerging sexuality will manifest itself as social and not natural.

But given that for Rousseau the adolescent's emerging sexuality sufficiently explains the rise of a social interest in others, his point is that this interest will involve the observation of others, the comparison of oneself with them and subsequently the competitive passions. What is unavoidable in this social interest is the loss of the adolescent's natural self-love (*amour de soi*) as a result of the observations and comparisons he now makes.

Extend these ideas, and you will see from where our *amour-propre* derives the form which we consider natural; and how *amour de soi*, ceasing to be an absolute sentiment, becomes pride in great souls, vanity in small ones, and in all nourishes itself incessantly at the expense of our neighbour. The essence of these passions, not having its germ in the heart of children, cannot grow there of itself; it is we who plant it there, and these passions would never take root except through our fault; but it is no longer so with the heart of the young man: whatever we may be able to do, they will grow there despite us. It is therefore time to change our method. (p. 250)

What Rousseau appears to be saying is that the social interest in others, arising out of sexual desire, necessarily involves the transformation of one's absolute self-love (*amour de soi*) into a relative one, relative in the sense that one's well-being for oneself in this self-love depends now on the observations and comparisons that one makes of others in relation to oneself. One's self-love acquires its social form in *amour-propre* and hence generates all the vicious and competitive passions. Clearly the new method of education that it is now necessary to undertake must prevent the generation of the evil passions, but however Rousseau proceeds from here it would seem that nature will have been entirely left behind, so that his project to refound society on nature will have to be abandoned. Nature has been lost in so far as *amour de soi* has been transformed into the non-natural and artificial *amour-propre*, and in so far as we now have a concern on the part of the adolescent for others and his relations to them which nature was seen to exclude. Man was presented as by nature self-sufficient and concerned only with himself, while this idea of the natural self-sufficiency of man was what determined the naturalness of the education that the child was given. So in introducing this 'unnatural' concern for others, from which the nature and extent of Emile's social relations develop, it would look as though Rousseau must abandon his project for an education in accordance with nature and must reject nature for society.

However, what we immediately find is not this, but the abandonment of his conception of the natural self-sufficiency of man.

It is man's weakness which makes him sociable; it is our common miseries which carry our hearts towards humanity: we would owe it nothing if we were not men. Every attachment is a sign of insufficiency: if each one of us had no need of others, he would hardly dream of uniting himself to them. Thus from our very infirmity is born our fragile happiness. A truly happy being is a solitary one; God alone enjoys an absolute happiness; but which of us has an idea of it? If some imperfect being could be sufficient for himself, what could he enjoy in our terms? He would be alone, he would be miserable. I do not conceive that he who has no need of anything can love anything: I do not conceive that he who loves nothing can be happy. (p. 259)

If man by nature is now said to need a relation with others through an attachment to them, this calls in question Rousseau's whole previous argument both of the *Discourse* and of *Emile*. For in the *Discourse* society was held not to be natural to man in so far as there was nothing in man's nature, as it appeared in a state of nature in its original condition, which in constituting a deficiency in the individual's life for himself required the presence of others to remove. And in *Emile* the child's education is supported by the ideas of the naturalness of individual human self-sufficiency. If this is false, then the whole previous argument is false, and it would appear that we must start again from the beginning. But we receive no acknowledgement at all by Rousseau of this difficulty, and he proceeds as though what he now says is fully compatible with everything that has gone before.

However, two points may be made against this quick identification of a radical inconsequence in Rousseau's argument. In the first place it might be argued that of course Rousseau does not take natural man of the *Discourse* or *Emile* the child to have completed humanity in themselves; they are radically incomplete and need the development of proper social relations for the fulfilment of their human nature. And secondly, the attachment to others that Rousseau now claims to be necessary for man's self-completion, is to be expressed through pity, which in the *Discourse* was presented as a natural sentiment possessed by natural man, so that the new departure is not really new but only a development of the old. Taking the second point first: pity in natural man had nothing to do with natural man's self-incompleteness and need for others; it did not affect the essence of his relations to others for it did not change the fact that he lived for himself alone. Pity in natural man was a super-fluous good, whereas pity, as it is now introduced as an attachment to others, arises out of the essential incapacity of man to be alone for himself. In view then of what Rousseau at this point says about pity, this pity could not have been experienced by man in a state of nature, for it reflects a conception of man as naturally lacking in self-sufficiency and so a conception which is radically different from and opposed to the old. This also concludes the first point; for while it is clear that Rousseau conceives of human nature as fully developed only in a properly arranged social condition, and thus assumes that natural man and the child are not fully developed men, nevertheless the sense in which they were said to embody nature at all, to be living a life according to that nature, was that of existing absolutely for themselves and not in their relations with others. And the paradox with which Rousseau opens *Emile* only makes sense on this basis: it is because by nature man lives for himself alone that society can be seen as requiring the denaturing of man by forcing him to live for others; whereas if we are now to say with Rousseau that man's nature requires him to attach himself to others, through love or pity, then the paradox is not resolved but abolished by sub-stituting for the initial premise, which produced the paradox, another with which the conclusion is entirely compatible.

This need for others, presented as a consequence of man's natural insufficiency, contradicts Rousseau's previous conception of man's nature. But the introduction of this new assumption cannot be accounted for in terms of Rousseau's need to explain the move-ment from nature to society. For we have already had this accounted for in terms of sexual desire, while this new assumption would not provide an account of the transformation from nature to society at all, since it abolishes the old nature and substitutes a new. Its point in the argument then is not to explain how men have a social interest, but to explain the particular form which Rousseau wishes this social interest to take in Emile, as an essential part of his strategy to accommodate the concern for others in *amour-propre*, and to make this concern productive of good both for Emile and for others. Thus while the original basis for the social interest is sexual desire, Emile is not to become immediately a lover. Rather, the expansiveness of his soul towards others, arising out of his emerging sexuality, is to be used for the creation of other relations. Consequently everything must be done to delay the adolescent's awareness of his developing sexuality, so that its outgoing energies can be directed into other channels. The aim, by prolonging his sexual innocence, is to 'profit from his growing sensibility, by injecting into the heart of the young adolescent the first seeds of humanity' (p. 258). The first seeds of humanity here are the feelings of pity and benevolence towards others, and these are to constitute the content of his introduction to, and first relations with, others. So what Rousseau has to account for is the possibility of the adolescent's first movement towards others taking this form. How he accounts for it is in terms of this natural insufficiency and corresponding natural need for an attachment to others arising out of our common nature as sufferers. It is because this natural insufficiency is expressed in our suffering that the spontaneous expression of this need for others will take the form of pity for their suffering.

Thus in the continuation of the last-quoted passage Rousseau says this:

It follows from this that we attach ourselves to our fellow men less through the sentiment of their pleasures than through the sentiment of their suffering; for we see much better in the latter the identity of our nature and the guarantee of their attachment for us. If our common needs unite us by interest, our common miseries unite us by affection. The aspect of a happy man inspires in others more envy than love; one would willingly accuse him of usurping a right which he does not have, by enjoying an exclusive happiness; and *amour-propre* suffers also because we are made to feel this man has no need of us. But who is there who does not commiserate with the unhappy man he sees suffering? Who is there who would not wish to deliver him from his ills, if a wish were to suffice for it? The imagination puts us in the place of the miserable rather than the happy; we feel that the former condition touches us more closely than the latter. Pity is sweet because in putting ourselves in the place of the sufferer, we nevertheless feel the pleasure of not suffering like him. Envy is bitter, in that the aspect of a happy man, far from putting the envious in his place, makes him regret not being there. It seems that the former exempts us from the ills which he suffers, and that the latter deprives us of the goods he enjoys. (pp. 259–60)

On this argument men naturally express their need for others through pity for their suffering, so that the adolescent can be expected to respond in this way. On this account also men are naturally sufferers. But Rousseau's view had been quite the contrary: that men naturally in their self-sufficiency will be quite content, and only social man inevitably suffers. Furthermore, Emile's education has been conceived in terms of the idea that in allowing him to retain his natural self-sufficiency, one will have ensured his happiness. Thus together with the assumption of natural self-sufficiency we have thrown out also the idea of man's natural happiness. As a result we have a basis for the construction of a new social consciousness founded in the cooperative passions of pity and benevolence, rather than in the competitive passions of pride and envy. But in terms of the overall argument the means of achieving this result can hardly be considered satisfactory.

The value of pity in the above passage is seen from the point of view of the pitier and not the sufferer. It is introduced as the way in which our need for others is most naturally expressed, and so its value consists in the satisfaction of this need. It satisfies us by providing us with a relation to another through the identification of ourselves with the suffering other, and by giving us pleasure arising out of the comparison we make between our own state and the state of the other. This in the first place is rather a peculiar account of pity, since it makes use of a sentiment of which the natural direction and primary concern is towards the relief of the suffering other, as a primary means of relieving oneself. But more striking is the fact that Rousseau presents pity as the way in which our need for an attachment to others is most naturally expressed. For of course one is inclined to say this need, now that it is given by Rousseau as a natural need, is naturally expressed and satisfied in the first place in the family, and later through the wider social relations of play, work and love. One is inclined to say that in normal circumstances it will be in these relations, through which we are present to others and others present to ourselves, that we seek and realize our attachments, and that pity for others, while not excluded, is something in which we find satisfaction over and beyond these primary attachments. It would seem that a man, whose primary attachment to others is pity for their suffering, must be a man deprived of all the normal ways in which we are attached to and exist for others, and that it is out of the suffering consequent upon his loneliness that he seeks his primary relation in identifying with other sufferers.

But if this is so, this condition of loneliness, given again that a relation to others is a natural need, is precisely the condition of one who, like Emile, has been brought up according to the new principles to be alone in human society, to think of himself without relation to others, so that he will not exist for others nor others for him. Emile the child is of course supposed to be happy in his aloneness, for he is supposed to be by nature self-sufficient; but since with adolescence he suddenly becomes by nature insufficient for himself, his carefully nurtured apartness from others will constitute an extreme loneliness in which pity for others may appear as the natural way to seek an attachment to them. But the conception of this whole process as natural can only be sustained if it is held that the child is naturally self-sufficient, which self-sufficiency is naturally lost in adolescence. This is not, however, the way in which Rousseau expresses it. His education for the child is deliberately aimed at securing the child's self-sufficiency on the grounds that man not the child is by nature self-sufficient, and his present account of the role of pity is founded on the supposition that man not the adolescent is by nature lacking in self-sufficiency. It is obvious that the child need not be self-sufficient in the way Rousseau's educational principles require, but could depend on his attachments to his family. And in so far as Rousseau's educational aim is to prevent this happening, we cannot now say unambiguously that the reason for this is to preserve nature, for Rousseau does not unambiguously consider man's nature to involve self-sufficiency. The role of the new education in Rousseau's whole social programme then becomes much clearer. For the basis for the new social consciousness, which will regenerate man and society, requires that pity for others should be the way in which we are primarily attached to them. This aim, however, will be defeated if the adolescent has already acquired, as his primary attachments, relationships with his family and others, which are based on sentiments other than pity, and through which he identifies himself as not alone in the human world. The new education, by doing its best to ensure that the adolescent does not identify himself in any relations but exists alone as isolated individual in the world, will have prepared him to establish relations with others in the way required for the new social consciousness to take effect.

Emile's growing sensibility to others, then, the original source of which is his developing sexuality, is to be used to discover others through pity for their suffering:

In order to excite and nourish this growing sensibility, in order to guide it or follow it in its natural course, what have we to do, if not to offer to the young man objects, on which the expansive force of his heart can act, which enlarge him, and extend him over other beings, which make him everywhere find himself outside himself. (pp. 261-2)

This expansion of one's being over others through pity occurs because pity involves transporting ourselves outside ourselves and identifying us with the suffering animal, for we quit, Rousseau says, in a manner our own being in order to take on the being of the other, and it is not in ourselves but in the other that we suffer (p. 261). This expansion of one's being over one's fellow men, Rousseau adds, must take place with the least possible personal interest, so that there should be no vanity, emulation or glory intermingled with this movement of pity, none of those sentiments which force us to compare ourselves with others (p. 266). And yet personal interest of a sort is involved in this movement of the heart, for in justifying this whole procedure in terms of Emile's happiness, he says that because Emile is introduced to the social world in this way, he will be happier than other young men, who on entering the most distinguished society, will suffer greatly from the comparisons they will be forced to make between their own appearances and those of others. For Emile on the other hand,

If the first spectacle which strikes him is an object of sadness, the first return on himself is a sentiment of pleasure. In seeing from how many ills he is exempt, he feels himself happier than he had thought. He shares the suffering of his fellow men; but this sharing is voluntary and sweet. He rejoices at the same time in the pity which he has for their ills, and in the happiness which exempts him from them. (p. 270)

And further on in the same passage he says, 'commiseration must be a very sweet sentiment, because it gives evidence in our favour'

75

(p. 270). The 'first return on oneself' from one's extension over others gives pleasure which consists in one's being better off than the other on the one hand, and in the sweetness of the feeling of pity itself presumably because it gives evidence in our favour. But as this personal interest which one has in one's pity does not involve a competition with others to show one's superiority, it will not involve vanity, emulation or glory.

The aim of this introduction to others through pity for their suffering is to bring Emile to a love of humanity, ('in a word, teach your pupil to love all men, and even those who despise them' [p. 266]), but Rousseau goes on to say that this love must begin not immediately with the whole of humanity, but with particular beings, those who are close to Emile and show an identity in their natures. And it is only after Emile's identification with particulars has been cultivated that it will be possible for him 'to generalize his individual notions under the abstract idea of humanity, and to join to his particular affections those which can identify him with his species (p. 276). But this relation to particulars must still be supposed to occur in the form of an identification with them as in the relation of pity, and extension of one's own being over the other, so that one finds oneself in the other. If this were not the case, the relation achieved to particulars could hardly be generalized by extending it in the desired way to the whole of humanity. But that it is the case can be seen from the immediately following considerations.

Through this relation to particulars, Rousseau says, 'we have at last entered the moral order' (p. 278). And he goes on to give some brief reflexions on this moral order, largely contained in a note of importance. He begins by saying in the main text that, if this were the place, he would show how the moral conscience derives from these first movements of the heart towards others that Emile is experiencing; and how the notions of justice and goodness are not only abstract words, or pure moral beings formed by the understanding, but that they are the affections of the soul enlightened by reason; and how reason alone, independently of conscience, could not establish natural law, which on the contrary must be founded on a natural need of the human heart (p. 278). The note to this passage elaborates his meaning thus:

Even the precept: act towards others as we wish that others act towards us, has no true foundation other than in conscience and sentiment; for what precisely is the reason for acting, being myself, as though I were another, especially when I am morally certain of never finding myself in the same situation?; and who will reply that in following this maxim very faithfully, I will get others to follow it in their relations with me? The evil man gains his advantage from the honesty of the just and his own injustice; he is quite content that all the world should be just except himself. That arrangement, whatever one may say, is not very advantageous for good men. But when the force of an expansive soul identifies me with my fellow man, and when I feel myself so to speak in him; it is in order not to suffer myself that I wish him not to suffer; I interest myself in him for the love of myself and the ground of the precept lies in nature itself, which inspires in me the desire for my well-being wherever I may feel myself to exist. From which I conclude that it is not true that the precepts of natural law are founded on reason alone, they have a more solid and certain base. The love of men derived from the love of self (*amour de soi*) is the principle of human justice. The sum of all morality is given in the Gospel by that of the law. (p. 278-9)

In this passage Rousseau takes for granted that the fundamental maxim of the moral or natural law is to act towards others as we wish others to act towards us. His problem is not to establish that this is the law we ought to follow, but in showing that we have a motive for following it. What is involved in the fundamental maxim is that I should apply a rule or principle of behaviour impartially to myself and others, so that the benefits I obtain from the application of the rule in my case I must grant to others when the application of the rule favours them. However, the application of the maxim requires altruistic action, action directed at benefiting another, and so a radical departure from purely, but innocently, self-interested nature. The question is as to how it is possible to depart from nature and acquire a motive for action directed at the good of another. Rousseau's answer is that by self-expansion into the other, I feel myself in him and make his interest mine, so that it is for my own sake (identified with the other) that I pursue his good. But the question still remains: how do I come to identify myself with the other in this way? is it something that, given a certain education, will occur naturally, or something that I can determine myself to, and so must have a motive for? Rousseau

77

certainly believes that if my innocent egoism is preserved until adolescence, and if I am then introduced to others only through pity for their suffering, I will naturally develop this capacity to extend my being over others and feel myself in them. But this extension is evoked by the suffering of others, so that where the maxim of morality is to be applied and no suffering is involved, the relevant feelings will be absent and some other motive will be required.

Rousseau's problem here as to the essentially moral motive is determined by his beginning with naturally 'good' egoism – the absolute existence of the I – and his seeking a transition from this condition to a sense of the individual's existence relative to others that will avoid the corrupting influence of *amour-propre*. For this excludes one obvious way in which children can learn to act altruistically, for the benefit of others. The child learns to act in this way for his parents through the desire to please them, and this desire itself is evoked by the child's sense of the importance to him of his relation to his parents. It would then be for the sake of the relation that the child acts to benefit his parents. But, however this motive, initially developed within the family, might be extended to cover larger and larger groups, it is a totally unacceptable motive to Rousseau. It is the desire to please another as the motive for one's action that is at the root of *amour-propre*, and that creates the corrupting dependence of men on each other.

Hence an alternative account is needed to avoid the operation of this motive, and we can at least see in the light of this negative reason something of Rousseau's purpose. Rousseau's alternative involves this self-identification with others, which he claims derives from natural self-love, from *amour de soi*. One's self-extension over others must then in a sense preserve one's natural egoism, consist merely of an extension of its operation to include the new area, the bodies of others, in which it now exists. This obliterates the distinction between oneself and the other. In acting for the other, it is not as a particular person acting for the benefit of another particular person that one acts, and so having a particular existence for him. The actor is the same person as he for whom the actor acts. Only one person exists in the transaction, who is at the same time oneself and the other. The problem of otherness, of what motive one can have for acting so as to benefit a different other, seems to be over-come without recourse to the corrupt motive by recreating oneness.

It is no doubt still obscure as to what exactly is involved in this oneness, and also how, apart from encouraging its development through pity for the suffering of others, it is to be brought about. This will have to be explored further when Rousseau's account of Emile's sense of his relative existence has been more fully developed. But for the moment we have here an initial understanding of the form that the new moral and social consciousness is to take. Central to it is a special interpretation of the fundamental moral maxim: act towards others as we wish others to act towards us. The maxim is defined so as to involve acting as though I were another, acting as though his good were mine, and it thus requires the new conscious-ness as an integral and substantive part of its elucidation. The maxim cannot be seen merely as a formal principle requiring impartial adherence to rules the content of which is left undetermined, a for-mal principle which cannot of itself establish the desirability or undesirability of a Rousseauan self-consciousness. The new con-sciousness is made to appear the only true moral stance, so that to take up the point of view involved in the moral maxim is to be already committed to a substantive position.

According to this first account of the new consciousness the love of others is said to derive from *amour de soi*. What then has happened to *amour-propre*? When Rousseau first considered Emile's awakening to the existence of others, he appeared to be saying that with the emergence of a social interest in Emile *amour de soi* would inevitably be transformed into *amour-propre* (see p. 69 above). But in the account of the new love of others derived from *amour de soi* there is no mention of, and appears to be no place for, *amour-propre*. And yet he has no sooner made the claim that the love of men derives from *amour de soi*, than *amour-propre* is reintroduced thus:

Up to the present Emile has considered only himself. The first look he gives his fellow men leads him to compare himself with them; and the first sentiment that this comparison excites in him is the desire for the first place. Here is the point at which *amour de soi* transforms itself into *amour-propre*, and at which all the passions which depend on the latter begin to grow. But to determine whether those passions which will predominate in his character will be humane and gentle, or cruel and evil, whether they will be the passions of benevolence and commiseration, or of envy and covetousness, it is necessary to know what position he will feel himself to occupy among men, and what sort of obstacles he might think that he will have to overcome in order to arrive at the position he wishes to occupy. (p. 279)

Rousseau's position in this passage reverts to the previous argument in that with Emile's first observation of others go comparisons between himself and others, which necessarily involve the transformation of *amour de soi* into *amour-propre*. With this transformation the vicious and competitive passions become possible dangers, so that Emile with his new interest in others has lost his natural innocence. Nevertheless *amour-propre* is held here to be capable of generating the good and cooperative passions as well as the vicious and competitive ones. The new method, which Rousseau has claimed is now necessary, obviously involves ensuring that it will be the good and not the bad passions that result from the transformation of *amour de soi* into *amour-propre*. The initial problem that this passage presents, however, is that *amour-propre* has hitherto been identified with the corrupt social world, as an artificial product of that world, having no foundation in nature. The good passions were presumed to derive from *amour de soi* and only the evil ones from *amour-propre*. This was the argument of the *Discourse* and is also specifically stated in *Emile*: 'we can thus see how the gentle and affectionate passions grow from *amour de soi*, and how the malignant and irascible passions grow from *amour-propre*' (p. 249). Clearly *amour-propre* in our present passage has been revalued, so as to make it ambivalent between the good and the bad passions. Since both can be engendered by *amour-propre* we cannot identify it with either, and since the set of passions which will predominate is said to depend on the judgements Emile makes as to his relation to other selves, we must interpret *amour-propre* in this passage as meaning the love of self, where the well-being of this self is dependent on the judgements made as to the relation between it and other selves. If the judgements are of one sort, the vicious passions will be engendered, and if of another the good passions will result. But while we now have to understand *amour-propre* as not inherently corrupting, the further problem remains that in so far as *amour de soi* is inevitably transformed into *amour-propre*, and the good social passions, on which the new moral order is based, derive from the latter and not from the former, Rousseau's assertion that the love of others in this new order is founded upon *amour de soi* is immediately contradicted. Furthermore, in respect of the view that the moral order is based on *amour-propre*, this order can no longer be held to be based on nature.

We have then up to this point a rather confused position, but before it is possible to attempt to dispel this confusion, it is necessary to proceed with the argument that continues from the reintroduction of *amour-propre* as the form in which social man inevitably experiences his self-love. The question posed by the passage is what judgements are necessary for the generation of the good passions, or what position in relation to others is it necessary for Emile to feel himself to occupy in order to become good for others while remaining good for himself. Rousseau immediately says that after having introduced Emile to others 'through the accidents common to the species' (p. 279), it is now necessary to introduce him to men in respect of their differences, by which he means 'natural and civil inequality, and the picture of the whole social order' (p. 279). The introduction of Emile to others that has already occurred through the 'accidents common to the species' was an introduction to them as sufferers, which through pity for the sufferer was supposed to produce the identification of Emile with the suffering other. This relation involves the making of judgements since the pleasure I have in feeling myself in him comes from my identifying him as worse off than myself, and so from feeling myself to be better off than he (see quotation p. 72 above). This is the comparison and judgement of *amour-propre*, but it is supposed to engender the love of others through the emotions of benevolence and compassion, and a total identification of oneself with the other.

We are left with the judgements Emile is to make in respect of the inequalities between men in the social order. Regarding these inequalities Rousseau says that while in a state of nature there is a real and indestructible equality between men, because each man is independent of the others, the equality of rights, which in civil society is supposed to be substituted for this natural equality, is chimerical and vain, because the public force is always used to favour the rich and powerful and oppress the weak. The multitude is always sacrificed to the few, and the public interest to private interest. The orders of civil society which are supposed to be useful for others are useful only to their own members, and are consequently against reason and justice. Having thus dismissed for Emile this particular problem, Rousseau says that it remains to be seen whether those who occupy the superior ranks are at least happy in their condition in order to know what judgement each man, and Emile in particular, is to make concerning his own lot. The answer will determine Emile's decision as to what place he is to occupy in society, and to know this he must begin by knowing the human heart (p. 280).

What Emile is required to learn is that 'man is naturally good' (p. 281) and that 'society depraves and corrupts men' (p. 281). At this point and from this point of view Rousseau recommends a study of history, so that Emile can acquire an understanding of the various passions of the heart, without having to get involved in the corruption of present society and so become accustomed in his own life to the spectacle of vice. The best history is one that presents only the facts, and leaves the reader to make his own judgements. Emile is also to observe his contemporaries, but the point with regard to the observation of both past and present men is that he should come to understand and judge them correctly without desiring to occupy any place other than his own. The danger is that 'as soon as *amour-propre* is developed, the relative self comes into play unceasingly, and the young man never observes others without returning on himself, and comparing himself with them' (p. 290), and that as a result he will desire to be other than he is. Yet Rousseau is confident that Emile will not take this last step, that he will be able to understand the effect opinion has on others without experiencing its dominion over himself, and that he will see the movement of passions in others without having his own heart disturbed by them. Emile, for Rousseau, interests himself in his brothers, is just and judges his equals, and if he judges them well, he will not wish to be in the position of any of them. And this is because the aim of all the torments, which according to Rousseau they give themselves, is founded on prejudices which Emile does not have, and which will appear to Emile as vain. For what Emile wants for himself is all within his own reach. He depends on no one, but is sufficient for himself and free of prejudices. Nurtured in the most absolute liberty, and believing that servitude is the worst of evils, he will commiserate with rather than envy the great and powerful, who in all their various ways are slaves, subject to those who obey them, to reputation or to their own opulence (p. 292).

In getting to know the various passions of men, and learning through the observation and judgement of others how society depraves and corrupts, Emile is supposed in returning on himself from his observations to be content with himself and not to covet another's place. But there remains the danger of his feeling proud of his superiority to others. To guard against this, Rousseau requires that Emile be humbled by allowing him to enter society and experience in himself the weakness and follies of the human heart. But of course his educator should be in close attendance to prevent things going too far and to ensure that he will learn from his mistakes.

The point of these observations and experiences of Emile is that he should be able to compare himself with others in respect of the inequalities in the social order, which give some superior positions to others, and yet not desire to be anybody other than himself. The basis for his self-contentment, however, is not that he is satisfied with the particular position in the social hierarchy that he actually occupies, for we are not in any case told what this position is. Rather, is its basis found in the judgement that, while those occupying superior positions are all in one way or another slaves of opinion and the competitive passions, he is free and in this respect better off than they. Here, then, the self that is loved in *amour-propre* is, as a result of the above comparisons, identified as occupying a superior position to others. But since this position is not any actual social position at all, but a moral position independent of all social positions, and from the viewpoint of which such social distinctions are irrelevant, the satisfaction of his *amour-propre* that it provides does not involve him in any social competition or rivalry. It thus leaves it open for his actual social relations with others to be conducted in terms of that other comparison from which resulted pity for their suffering and total identification with them. We have, that is to say, two ways in which Emile is to compare himself with others. In the first he compares himself with others in respect of human suffering, and judges himself to be better off, but also to possess at the same time a common nature as sufferer; while in the second he compares himself with others in respect of the social distinctions and judges himself to be better off by virtue of being above all such distinctions. But while the former comparison and judgement can serve as the basis for what Rousseau conceives as an order of relations with others, namely relations constituted by an identification of selves, the latter involves only a rejection of the social order of inequality as being irrelevant, and puts nothing in its place. What is to be put in its place is the order resulting from the first comparison.

Thus after having explained how Emile is to be content with himself in the face of the opulence of others, Rousseau says that Emile must also live in the world, and the occupation in the world that Rousseau gives him is that of humanitarianism, what Rousseau calls the exercise of the social virtues (p. 299). His interest in the world is to be the interest of the poor, whom he is to assist with his money and his attentions, and to whom he is to devote his person and his time. He is to become indeed a knight errant penetrated with a tender love of humanity (p. 302). This actual relation to others Rousseau now generalizes thus:

Extend *amour-propre* over others, we will transform it into virtue, and there is no human heart in which this virtue does not have its root. The less the object of our cares concerns ourselves immediately, the less the illusion of particular interest is to be feared; the more one generalizes this interest, the more just it becomes; and the love of the human race is in us nothing other than the love of justice. Do you wish then that Emile love the truth, do you wish him to know it; make him in his activities exist outside himself. The more his attentions are devoted to the happiness of others, the more enlightened and wise they will be, and the less will he be mistaken in what is good or evil; but never allow him any blind preference, founded solely on partiality or unjust prejudice. And why should he harm one in order to serve another? It little matters to him who obtains a larger share of happiness, provided that it serves the greatest happiness of all: that is the first interest of the wise man after his private interest; for each man is part of his species and not of another individual. (p. 303)

In this passage a generalization of the individual's interest is held to produce a general good or greatest happiness of all which is identified with justice and the love of the human race. If the generalization of individual interest is to produce justice, the idea would seem to be that of arriving at an interest of the individual which as the generalization is extended becomes common to a larger and larger number of people. The limit to this extension would be what is reached through universalization of individual interest, when the individual pursues as his interest only what is an interest for all men. This idea of universalizing one's interest to arrive at a common interest for all men, the pursuit of which is justice, seems to be what Rousseau is developing.

This common interest arises when *amour-propre* is extended over others. It may be wondered whether Rousseau means *amour-propre* here rather than *amour de soi*, since it is not clear that it makes any sense at all for an individual to extend his *amour-propre* over others. For if we understand by *amour-propre* love of the self in its existence relative to others, the distinction between the self and others is built into it and renders meaningless the idea of loving others as we love ourselves (*amour-propre*). But if we take *amour-propre* to involve the demand for preference or superiority for oneself, then the extension of this demand to others would require the same preference being given to others as to oneself, which in effect amounts to equality as between oneself and others. The conclusion is an equal right for all, which seems also the content of the common interest arrived at by universalization of individual interest, and again to be what is involved in the earlier account of the derivation of the moral consciousness from self-love (*amour de soi*).

We ought now to be in possession of the central elements of Rousseau's solution to the social problem. The fundamental requirement for such a solution was that men should be related to each other in a social existence in a way that did not involve their particular identity and value for themselves being dependent on the particular identity and value they had for others. In so far as *amour-propre* represented a concern for this relative existence and value, it must be done away with in favour of some form of *amour de soi* through which in nature one has only an absolute existence and value for oneself. But as we have seen, both *amour-propre* and *amour de soi* are involved in Rousseau's solution.

Amour-propre emerges as soon as the adolescent awakens to the existence of others and begins to make judgements as to how he exists relative to them. But by concentrating those judgements on relative suffering we can evoke in the adolescent the benevolent rather than the competitive passions, and engender that relation of identification between himself and suffering others which is seen as the foundation of the moral order. By extending his being over the suffering other and identifying himself with the sufferer, the differentiation between pitier and sufferer is overcome and a common identity, a oneness, is attained. This relation to another whereby the differentiating particularity of oneself and the other is overcome through the recreation of the oneness of nature is developed further in the new moral order. Here one arrives through universalization of one's individual interest at an interest or good of one's own which is at the same time common to all. This common interest or good again serves to obliterate the distinction between self and others. The essential feature of the common good from this point of view is that it is one and the same good for oneself and others. Hence in pursuing this good one can pursue it equally as one's own or as the good of others without concern for this distinction. In pursuing one's own good one is pursuing theirs, or in pursuing their good one is pursuing one's own.

The essence of the solution, both in respect of pity for the suffering other and in respect of the common good, consists in the abolition of the different goods of self and others and the recovery of a single good common to both. Thus the solution can be said to be based on nature, since it is always and only one good and identity that has to be pursued, so that this good exists absolutely for itself and not relatively to some other different good. The individual always has as his end such an absolute good. At the same time the solution depends on the transformation of the original principle of nature – *amour de soi* – into *amour-propre*, since the self must become concerned with its relative existence for the solution to take effect. However, the judgement that the self must make is that it has essentially the same identity and interest as other selves (as fellow sufferer or fellow man). This judgement ensures that how one sees oneself as related to another does not include the differentiating particularity of oneself or the other. It is not as a particular person with a particular identity and value that one is related to others, but only as undifferentiated fellow man or fellow sufferer.

Although in this way the relative judgements of *amour-propre* are a necessary element in the reformed social man's consciousness, and although self-identification through these relative judgements involves a form of dependence on others, no corruption can occur. Dependence on others is involved, since the self's new identity and interest can only be acquired through its relation to others. The self exists only relative to the common identity and interest. However, this dependence is radically different from the dependence Rousseau has identified as essentially corrupting. Corrupting dependence consisted in the individual's concern for his *particular* identity and value relative to others, his concern how as a differentiated particular he was identified and valued by differentiated others. Since this involved an inherent conflict between the different values accorded to different men, the gain in value of one only being possible through the reduction in value of others, the concern for relative particularity set men against each other and produced an essentially competitive consciousness. This form of dependence, however, is excluded when the object of the individual's concern in his relations with others is not his *particular* good or *particular* identity but a *common* good and *common* identity. The advancement of the good of one is the advancement of the good of all. No one can gain at another's expense.

The above solution to the social problem involves a reconciliation between *amour-propre* and *amour de soi*, between nature and society. But it depends on the individual making one kind of relative self-identification rather than another. Why should the individual have as the object of his relative concern his common identity and interest as fellow man or fellow sufferer, rather than as differentiated particular man? That he ought to have the former as the object of his concern, that the former is the only possible moral stance is clearly what Rousseau believes. So we at least know what the solution to the social problem formally consists in. But if there is no motive for the individual to adopt this stance and to identify himself in the required manner, and every motive for the individual to continue or readopt the old corrupt stance and identification, the formal solution will be of little actual relevance for human affairs. Here we return to the question of the motive for adopting the new moral point of view. Why should the individual not be concerned with his particular value for others?

In the first place the education of the child should have ensured that until adolescence no such concern for his particular value for others could have entered his consciousness. He remains the natural egoist. Subsequently, however, when the adolescent becomes aware of others, the positive inclination to identify himself with them seems to rest entirely on a posited lack of self-sufficiency or weakness in the individual which draws him towards suffering others. But being attracted to the suffering of others does not itself involve the required identification with them, nor is it necessarily a reason for it. For as a provider of services to the sufferer one acquires a particular value for him, and this could be the object of one's concern. Indeed Rousseau recognizes some such element at work in the operation of pity. One both feels the other has need of one, and senses that one is better off than he (see p. 72 above). But this makes the motive for the required identification with the sufferer the corrupt *amour-propre*, whether this is understood to be the desire to be of particular value for another or the desire to be of superior value to him.

Furthermore, in order to arrive at the moral stance a move is necessary from the individual's identification with the sufferer to his identification with all men as men. Here nothing positive appears to be offered at all as the motive for it, other than the implication of a natural extension of a habit first acquired in respect of feelings of pity for suffering others. However, we do find again a reference to the corrupt *amour-propre*, as support for the moral stance, in Emile's judgement that he is superior to others on the grounds of their slavish subjection to the tyranny of opinion contrasted with his freedom (see pp. 83–4 above). In so far as to maintain this freedom in society it is necessary to adopt the moral stance, then the motive to adopt the latter which is being encouraged here is the sense of superiority it gives the individual. But this motive could only operate where there are others who have not yet adopted the same stance.

In any case the motives which are being appealed to both in respect of pity and the moral stance are of a morally corrupt nature, and are hardly consonant with the main direction of Rousseau's argument, which is aimed at showing how the right moral attitude towards others can, given the correct education, be made to develop quite naturally from the feelings of the individual. If we ignore these morally dubious motives one might suppose a strong negative reason for identifying oneself in the required way, and for not having as the object of one's concern one's particular value for others. This would be the desire to avoid the anxiety arising from uncertainty as to one's valuation by others and the fear of being valued at a very low rate. But such a motive could only exist for those who wished to avoid the strains of dependence and competition. For those who accepted them, there would be no attractions in the new morality. It would also be a motive of no great worth.

Is all this largely beside the point? The essential point is rather that the only way in which the individual can both maintain the original principle of his nature and exist for others, be at the same time good for himself and others, is by universalizing his identity and good and by having as his concern this common identity and common good. Education if skilfully carried through ensures that the individual will come to feel that his good lies in following this way, and that concern for his particular value for others will be repugnant to him. This is indeed Rousseau's argument. However, the trouble consists precisely in the dependence of success on a skilful education. What the skill is required for is to counteract the very strong tendency for child and adolescent to develop a concern for their particular value for others. This attraction of the individual towards the corrupt relation is indeed on Rousseau's own argument so strong that it appears as a second nature. In the *Discourse* corruption comes so to speak naturally to man as soon as he finds himself living together with others. It is not some few evil persons who are responsible for corruption, but all who spontaneously embrace it, while in *Emile* the continuous concern of the educator during childhood is to prevent the child becoming aware of his relative existence, since it is assumed that such an awareness would immediately produce the corrupt motive. And when the awareness does come with adolescence, so at once does the corrupt desire.

Furthermore this concern for one's particular value for others would seem the natural and immediate response of a being who has become conscious of his existence for others and his relation to them. His first concern is his particular value for himself. In becoming aware of having a particular identity for others a concern for it would seem to follow naturally. This 'natural' response must therefore be countered energetically. But by what? Rousseau should say by some other natural feeling. Hence the need to have a motive for adopting the moral position. But the only possible motive, apart from those discussed above, appears to be the belief engendered by education that this is the best position for the individual to adopt in society. The belief may be right, but its foundation in natural feeling is very uncertain.

Let us return to the question of the formal correctness of the solution. Whatever the difficulties may be in getting men to adopt it, they do not destroy the validity of Rousseau's solution. In so far as this solution is at all possible, Rousseau appears to have achieved what I claimed was impossible, namely the founding of a social consciousness on a conception or principle of nature which is essentially nonsocial. But the derivation of the new social consciousness from nature involves a significant contradiction in the account Rousseau gives of nature. For on the original account of nature in the *Discourse* man was said to be naturally self-sufficient, existing absolutely for himself alone and needing no relation to another. And it is this absolute self-sufficiency which constitutes the principle of nature that must be reproduced in a different form in society, in the form of a common good, rather than in the form of a single individual's good. But in order to show how the individual can be drawn towards

others through pity for their suffering, Rousseau argues that man
is naturally lacking in self-sufficiency and naturally needs a relation
to another. Both these accounts of nature are necessary for his
argument, the first in order to support the particular conception of
the social good that he develops, and the second in order to show
how men might be attracted towards it.[1] Since it was the first
account of nature, absolute self-sufficiency, that I claimed was
inherently non-social and incompatible with a social consciousness,
Rousseau's self-contradiction on just this point is support for my
original claim. Nevertheless if we left aside the question of man's
attraction towards others, and suppose man to be entirely self-
sufficient, we would still be left with an account of a social order,
which in some sense reproduces or is based on an inherently non-
social principle, and this seems incoherent. Hence there ought to be
something incoherent about the account of the new social order that
Rousseau gives us.

The crucial element in this new order is the reproduction of
nature through the recovery of oneness, the substitution of a single
common identity and common good for the multiplicity of identities
and goods involved in the distinction and separation of self and
other. Essential to this substitution is the idea of the self-identification of the individual with the other. I shall first examine the idea of
identification as it is supposed to hold between pitier and sufferer.

Pity is characterized by Rousseau as a relation to a particular
sufferer whereby the one who pities extends his own being over the
other and finding himself in the other, feels or suffers in him (pp.
261–2 and note, p. 278). The pitier identifies himself with the
sufferer so as to make the other's suffering his own. What sense can
be given to this idea of identification through pity? Since there are
two individual beings, specifically differentiated in respect of the
one suffering and the other not, how can identification take place?
It is true that as the basis of pity for another's suffering one must feel

[1] That I here suppose Rousseau to be basing the moral consciousness on the 'natural'
feeling of pity does not involve a contradiction of my argument of the previous section. The cultivation of pity is an essential *part* of Emile's moral development. The
issue of the previous section concerned the dubious attraction Rousseau supposed
pity had for men, and the insufficiency of pity alone to produce the full moral consciousness.

the other's condition as miserable and feel this for oneself. To do this one must imagine oneself in the other's position, and actually put oneself by thought into it. This imaginative identification of oneself with the other requires also that one feel oneself to be like the other, vulnerable in the same respect, a potential sufferer.

All this is compatible not only with feeling pity for the suffering other, but also with repulsion from his situation. The imaginative identification with the other cannot be itself pity, but only the necessary basis for it. What, then, does Rousseau suppose to be going on? As we have seen, the relation to another involved in pity for his suffering is presented as the foundation of the new moral order. It must constitute the foundation of a solution to Rousseau's social problem and so must be a relation to another which excludes the corrupt relation of dependence, in which each is concerned with, and dependent for his well-being on, the attitude of the other towards him as a particular being. How might concentration on the suffering of others be thought to provide what is desired? The great value of pity for the suffering of others in this respect is that it enables one to be good for others without apparently having to attend to their consciousness of or attitude towards oneself. One is thus in a position of doing good for others without having to act so as to please them and thereby without having to subject oneself to their judgement of one. This is achieved in so far as one can treat the needs of the sufferer as needs objectively given by his condition. In relating myself to his objectively given needs, I can make the satisfaction of these the end of my action without making the pleasing of the person whose needs they are my end. I pursue his needs not as *his* needs, but as merely the needs of a suffering body. In this way I can make these needs my own and feel myself, so to speak, in his suffering. Hence it appears that his suffering is mine, and the required identification has taken place.

But what has taken place is not an identification between myself and his suffering self, but rather a separation of his needs as suffering body from himself as a person and then the appropriation of these needs as mine. It is only by first of all denying the other's personal or subjective ownership of the needs, and so liberating them from his person, that I am enabled to make them mine, to feel them and pursue them as mine. It is thus false to say, as Rousseau does, that the pitier feels himself in the other. He feels himself in the other's body and can do so only by denying the other's ownership of it. In this there is no relation of identification achieved between oneself and another, for the relation begins with the denial of the other's person. There is merely oneself and the extension of oneself in the body of another. Nowhere is there an other for one.

My claim was that a social consciousness could not be founded upon the conception of nature that we find in Rousseau, since that nature was defined in terms of existing for oneself alone. Now we find that the foundation of the new social order in the relation of pity for the suffering of another turns out in fact to involve the denial of the other and the appropriation of his suffering as a means of one's extension outside oneself. The principle of nature is indeed preserved, but no social relation between persons presented. Such a relation is claimed but does not exist. Instead we have as the foundation of the new order the radical corruption of pity.

For the value of pity consists precisely in what Rousseau denies – not, that is, simply in attention to objectively given needs, but in attention to the subjective condition of the sufferer. Pity involves making the sufferer feel that it is precisely *his* suffering that is the object of one's concern. It is the feeling of a person who is not suffering for another *person* in his suffering. It requires the differentiation between the person of the pitier and the person of the sufferer, such that the pitier has as the object or end of his feeling and action the relief of the other. The satisfaction of the other is the object of the pitier's concern, so that in acting for his sake the pitier subordinates himself to the other's response. In existing in the relation of pity to please the other, one makes oneself dependent on the other in precisely the way identified by Rousseau as corrupt.

We have next to consider the nature of the common good that Rousseau must be supposing to arise from the universalization of one's individual interest.

The essence of this movement of the self and its interest as a solution to Rousseau's social problem was seen to lie in the fact that what was generated was *one* good which was the same for all individuals. Thus although the common good involves individuals' dependence on one another, since each is only part of the whole, this is not a corrupting dependence since, being the same for all, it excludes differentiation and division. I can pursue the common good as *my* good without seeking this as a good pertaining to a being which is differentiated and distinguished from others. Each in pursuing the common good for himself is necessarily pursuing the same good for others at the same time.

The crucial fact for Rousseau about the common good is that it appears to exclude differentiation. But given that it is the same good for many different individuals, who may be supposed to have many different interests, what is the relation between this common good and the different private interests of the same individuals? Does the common good abolish or supersede the different individual interests? Since the initial problem for Rousseau arose out of the natural pursuit by each individual of his own private ends independently of others in circumstances in which one man's ends conflict with the ends of others, the common good would only have to supersede those different individual interests which conflict with each other. Provided that individuals can pursue their own ends independently of the ends of others and so without coming into conflict with them, then pursuit of such private ends is compatible with the pursuit of the common good. The common good would define the limits within which private ends can be pursued.

The pursuit of private ends that do not conflict with those of others would be directly in accordance with the original principle of nature, by which a man pursues his good absolutely without reference to others. The individual must of course make a prior reference to others in so far as he can only desire what is compatible with the common good and so their good also. But the common good, as we have seen, is also in accordance with the principle of nature. Hence the pursuit of the common good on the one hand and independent private ends on the other appears both coherent and fully in accord with nature.

The difficulty with this theory is that it is incapable of accounting satisfactorily for conflicts between private ends that are at the same time compatible with the common good. There is no reason why such conflicts could not occur and every likelihood that they will. For if the common good is fundamentally the same and so an equal right for all, to be arrived at through universalization of individual interest, and if the interest of the individual is the liberty to pursue his own ends without interference by or dependence on others, then all the common good prescribes, in respect of the ends the individual can choose, is that they must be compatible with the equal right of others to pursue their ends. But this in no way excludes the possibility or even the probability of the exercise of the equal right leading to a conflict between the end of one man and the end of another.

There exists no possibility within Rousseau's conception of the principle of nature of doing anything about such conflicts, other than declaring that the ends which produce them are the products of the corrupted will and so cannot legitimately be desired. For the only way in which such conflicts can be sensibly resolved is through the operation of what for Rousseau is the spirit of corrupt dependence. There must be a compromise between the conflicting parties. Each must desire a particular arrangement of the differences between the various interests which all can accept as satisfactory to them. The arrangement will have as its substance a particular relation or set of relations between the various parties as differentiated particulars, not undifferentiated identities. The particular relation or set of relations to others is what each will have as his object, and so each will desire to exist for others in terms of this relation, having a particular value for them defined by it.

A different conception of the common good from that of Rousseau's is involved. The common good is not a relation between undifferentiated identities, men as pure men, but a relation between particular persons as they are differentiated from each other. The common good for a collection of persons and interests no doubt at an abstract level consists in peace, harmony, justice, but the concrete manifestation of such goods possessed in common by a particular collection of persons involves a particular set of relations between them expressing their differentiated existence and concerns. The spirit of compromise necessary to produce such a common good requires Rousseau's corrupt motive, namely the desire in each party to please the other, to find an arrangement acceptable to himself which will be acceptable also to the other. Each will be concerned with the particular value he has for the other, and so will become dependent in the corrupt way on him.

Thus for Rousseau's common good solution to work, conflicts between private ends that do not infringe an equal right for all must be overcome in some other way than through the spirit of compromise. But what other way is possible? Only the suppression of the desires which produce them on the grounds that they are the product of the corrupted self. Yet the grounds for holding that the particular ends that conflict are the product of the corrupted self are simply that they in fact conflict. This fact is purely accidental to them and has nothing to do with the nature of the desires themselves. Were the conflict by chance to be removed, the desire would immediately become innocent.[1]

Rousseau's idea of the common good is an attempt to solve the following problem: how is the individual to cease treating others merely as means or obstructions to his own ends, as he does in an innocent way in nature and childhood, without coming to treat the other as a particular end for him as someone besides himself for whom he exists and whom he seeks to please? The answer to the problem is for each to universalize his individual interest and so recognize the equal right of the other to pursue his ends. In recognizing this right one acknowledges his existence as an end for himself. But one does not thereby make him a particular end for oneself, a particular being whom one exists to please. For at the level at which one recognizes the other's claims, he has no particularity, he is an

---

[1] It might be argued that one way out of the difficulty of conflicting ends lies in the operation of perfectly competitive markets. Conflicts of ends are settled by competition and exchange. The competitive market preserves the independence of each person's ends. For each strives for the best bargain for himself relative to his system of ends, and uses what others can provide merely as means to the realization of this system. All must of course accept the basic rules of the market. But these can be seen as common interests of the Rousseauan kind, and so as what each desires for himself in order to preserve the independence of his ends. This free market philosophy does indeed seem entirely in accord with the basic principles of the Rousseauan philosophy of independence. However, it is *not* Rousseau's solution. It is also an account only of the relations that *may* exist between persons in a competitive market. There is no need for participants in a market to see others purely as means to their own ends.

abstract, undifferentiated individual. This is the level at which the other constitutes for one an end. But since at this level the other has no particular ends, exists only as an abstract pursuer of ends, in recognizing him one takes no notice of the particular ends he has. His particularity is entirely irrelevant to one's relation to him. So also is one's own particularity. Self and other are mere duplications of abstract individuality. Each abstract individual has of course his own system of particular ends. But provided that the particular ends of others do not impinge on one's own, provided they are independent, there will exist no relation between the particularity of the self and the particularity of the other. Each has his own particularity, but one man's exists as in nature only tangentially to another's.

Rousseau's solution requires the particularity of each to be related tangentially in this way. It must exclude the relation between particulars that comes into existence when one man's ends bear on another's, and when each recognizes the other as a particular end for him. This creates the need and desire for each to please the other, which constitutes the dependent and degenerate condition of man that Rousseau wishes to do away with. It is done away with to the extent that men are related to others only as abstract individuals having no particularity and so as identical with themselves, and to the extent that as particulars each exists for himself alone.

The effectiveness of this solution depends on what is to happen to the need and desire of the individual to have as his end not abstract individuals but real particulars, to the desire to exist for others in their particularity. The need for it arises with the impingement of individuals' ends on each other, and this is obviously great. The desire I have argued clearly appears from Rousseau's own argument as a strong spontaneous force in men. It also seems evident that such a desire is naturally expressed by the child in his love for and dependence on his parents, and is later extended to larger and larger groups to which he may belong.

The status of this desire is the crucial question. Rousseau holds that it is not natural to man, but the artificial product of society. That it is not natural to man in a state of nature is evident. For in the state of nature he knows no others, and so could not have the desire to exist for them. If, as soon as he knows others in society, the desire is evoked in him, then it does not seem to matter very much whether one says that the desire is the artificial product of society, where artificial gets its meaning from the contrast with the state of nature, or whether one says that the desire is natural for man to experience in society. But if the desire is not natural to man either in nature or in society, but only produced in him in society through an inadequate conception of the true nature of the self and of the moral relation to others, then once the adequate conception has been developed and accepted, the desire should disappear. This is what we should now expect Rousseau to believe will happen. Since for Rousseau man is naturally good, and only fortuitously and not necessarily corrupted in society, the new consciousness should altogether abolish the old.

However, if we accept, as seems obvious, that both the need and the desire for particular existence for others is inevitably developed in society, we should expect Rousseau's solution, by requiring the suppression of this desire, to create a permanent conflict within each man between what he will believe to be his moral will for an undifferentiated identity with others and his particular will for particular relations. Some such permanent split within men is precisely what we find coming to the surface as Rousseau develops his account of the moral personality.

FREEDOM

Having introduced Emile to other men and indicated how he ought to see himself in relation to them and the social order, Rousseau raises the question of what religious beliefs it is possible to incorporate into his idea of an education according to nature. What has to be excluded is any religion that requires for its adoption the authoritative instruction of others, so that Emile believes in the authority or opinion of others and not in the conviction of his own reason. If Emile is to have any religious beliefs, they must be ones that at the relevant stage in the development of his reason he is capable of grasping by and for himself. What Rousseau offers for Emile to believe at this point is given in the form of a profession of faith by a Savoyard vicar. The articles of this faith, however, are presented as the products of rational reflexion about the nature of the individual self and of the universe, and thus constitute beliefs available to the natural understanding unaided by divine inspiration or authoritative pronouncement. They form the content of what Rousseau calls a natural religion, a religion that all men can adhere to following their own inner convictions, without involving themselves in disputes over the different particular dogmas of different churches.

While the articles of the natural religion contain putative truths about the nature of God, the reasoning, which is aimed at establishing these, also leads into a conception of the dual nature of human beings. It is the development of this dualistic conception of human nature that is the subject of this section. My argument in the last section involved the claim that Rousseau's solution to his social problem would produce an internal conflict within each man between what he would have to see as an ideal existence of himself on the one hand (the moral will) and what he could possibly see as base reality on the other (particular will). This self-conflict we now find being given metaphysical expression in the form of the religious argument of the profession of faith and especially in the idea in this argument of free will.

The Savoyard vicar's enquiry begins with the question: who am I? The first answer is that 'I exist and have senses through which I am affected' (p. 325). But although the Savoyard vicar is thus certain of his own existence he is not immediately sure that the 'I' which constitutes *his* existence is simply the succession of his sensations or something independent of these. But of his sensations he is sure that they are his, i.e. that they occur in him, and at the same time that their cause is external to him, since, he says, it does not depend on himself whether he has these sensations or not. His sensation is to be distinguished from its cause or object. He thus arrives at his second truth, namely that something other than himself exists. This something he calls matter, and in so far as it exists in individual things he calls it bodies. We have then the existence both of himself and an external world composed in part of individual pieces of matter.

In reflecting on the objects of his sensation, he finds in himself the capacity to compare them and he says 'he feels himself endowed with an active power of which he was not previously aware' (p. 325). In sensation objects present themselves to him in a separate and isolated manner, as absolutely distinct, and it is only by comparing one object with another that he can begin to make judgements as to their relations, differences and similarities. This capacity of comparing and judging objects, which present themselves to him through sensation, does not belong to him as a being of pure sensation, for the content of these judgements is not given in sensation, but is something which he imposes on the objects. This capacity is the distinctive faculty of an active or intelligent being. A purely sensible being is an entirely passive being not endowed with intelligence. Consequently the nature of the 'I' about which there was an initial doubt must consist of something more than a succession of pure sensations. The individual must also have within him an active intelligent principle of being to be distinguished from his passive being as pure sensation, passive as it is merely produced by the objects of the external world (pp. 325–7).

Having assured himself of his own existence, the Savoyard vicar turns his attention to the nature of the external world, and observes the matter of which it is composed to be sometimes in movement and sometimes at rest. He infers from this that neither movement nor rest is essential to matter, but that movement must be the effect of a cause, of which rest is merely the absence. Thus, if nothing acts on matter, matter will be at rest. He then distinguishes two sorts of movement in bodies: communicated movement, where the cause of the movement is external to the object moving, and spontaneous or voluntary movement where the cause of the movement is internal to the object. His reason for saying that there are voluntary movements is not that he observes such movements in objects or beings external to him, but that he feels it to be true of himself; 'I wish to move my arm and I move it without this movement having any immediate cause other than my will' (p. 328). He himself, and by extension beings like himself, has the capacity to move himself by an act of will which is independent of any pressures exerted by objects in the external world. Matter on the other hand manifests no such capacity for self-movement, and since its natural condition is to be at rest, when it does move, it must have a cause external to it. Furthermore, the movement of matter occurs not in a random way, but according to constant laws. But since these laws are not themselves substances, and only determine the effects without revealing the causes, they do not suffice to explain the movement of the universe. The Savoyard vicar concludes then that the first cause of movement must be spontaneous or voluntary, the product of a will. This is his first principle, from which he deduces his first article of faith, namely that a will moves the universe and animates nature (p. 330).

How a will can produce a physical action the Savoyard vicar finds himself unable to answer other than by repeating that he experiences the connexion in himself. He feels it makes more sense than the supposition that an inanimate body moves itself. But he finds it no more possible to explain than to explain how his sensations could affect his soul. The mode of union between his active and passive nature appears to him absolutely incomprehensible. Nevertheless he feels that his first article of faith offers a sense which is repugnant neither to reason nor observation.

Moving matter requires the existence of a will as first cause, but matter moving according to certain laws shows that this will must also be an intelligent will. This is his second article of faith (p. 332). This intelligence is manifest in the order and harmony of the universe. The being who possessed this intelligent will, the creator of the universe, he calls God. The attributes of God are intelligence, power, will, and following necessarily from these, goodness. He knows that God exists, that God exists by Himself, and that, as author of all things, all things, including himself, are subordinated to God's existence. But beyond this he knows nothing of God. He sees God in all his works, feels God in himself, but as soon as he wishes to contemplate God Himself, to know what He is or what His substance is, God escapes him and he can no longer understand.

Returning from God to a consideration of himself and the place he occupies in the order of things, he observes that by his species he is' first in rank in the order of nature. For by his will and intelligence man disposes of his environment in a way which no other being on earth can. But when the Savoyard vicar comes to reflect on his individual place among men, he sees, as opposed to the order and harmony of nature, nothing but disorder and confusion. From here he arrives at a conception of the human soul.

He says:

In meditating upon the nature of man, I believed that I had discovered in it two distinct principles, of which one raised man to the study of eternal truths, to the love of justice and moral beauty, to the regions of the intellectual world the contemplation of which constitutes the delights of the wise man, and of which the other brought man back basely into himself, subjected him to the empire of the senses, to the passions that are their ministers, and contradicted through these everything that the sentiment of the former inspired in him. In feeling myself carried away, fought over by these two contrary movements I said to myself; No, man is not one: I will and yet do not will. I feel myself at the same time enslaved and free; I see the good, I love it, and I do evil; I am active when I listen to my reason, passive when my passions carry me away; and my worst torment when I succumb is to feel that I could have resisted. (p. 337)

In this passage the distinction initially drawn in the Savoyard vicar's self-contemplation, between the active and passive principle of being in man, is connected with a number of other distinctions, that between an intellectual world and the world of the senses, between good and evil, reason and the passions, freedom and slavery. Furthermore, these distinctions are presented as being experienced in man as necessarily opposed modes of being, so that man is not a unity, not even a complex unity, but an incoherent duality. This duality is manifest also in the opposition between man's natural inclination to give preference to himself before all else, and his innate love of justice. To suppose man to be formed of one simple substance, it is necessary to remove these contradictions (p. 338).

The Savoyard vicar offers an argument to support this conception of man as formed of two substances. By substance he means being endowed with some primitive quality in abstraction from all particular or secondary modifications of this quality. If all such primitive qualities could be united in one single being, then there would only be one substance; but if some primitive qualities mutually exclude each other, then there will be as many substances as there exist such mutual exclusions. He then takes it for granted that matter as such a primitive quality cannot think, while thinking beings also exist. Furthermore the mind of such thinking beings, although in man appearing to be located in matter, is essentially independent of it.

Something in you seeks to break the bonds which confine it; space itself is not your measure, the whole universe is not large enough for you: your sentiments, your desires, your anxiety, your pride even, have another principle than this narrow body in which you feel yourself imprisoned. (p. 339)

So man is composed of two essentially independent substances, mind and body. The independence of the substance mind is also manifest in the independence of the human will, which the Savoyard vicar expresses thus:

No material being is active by itself and I am. It is useless to dispute this with me, I feel it, and this sentiment which speaks to me is stronger than the reason which opposes it. I have a body on which other bodies act and which acts on them; this reciprocal action is not in doubt; but my will is independent of my senses; I consent or resist, I succumb or conquer, and I feel perfectly in myself when I do what I wished to do, or when I only yield to my passions. I always have the power of willing, not the force to execute that will. When I yield to temptations, I act according to the impulsion of external objects. When I reproach myself for this weakness, I listen only to my will; I am enslaved by my vices, and free by my remorse, the sentiment of my liberty is obliterated only when I become depraved and when I prevent the voice of the soul from raising itself against the law of the body. (pp. 339–40)

The human will, then, is essentially independent of the body in which it is located and is free. The question as to what determines the content of will is given the answer, human judgement. And judgement is determined by man's 'intelligent faculty' or his power of judging. And since this faculty is in the human being and not given to him from outside himself, the determining cause of his judgement and so his will is inside himself. Man is thus self-determining and free in his actions, and as such, the Savoyard vicar claims, he is animated by an immaterial substance, his soul, which is his third article of faith (p. 340).

Man, being free, is free to do evil as well as good. He alone is responsible for the evil that he does. The reason why God has given man this freedom cannot be known, but its value consists in the possibility it provides for man to attain the supreme joy of self-contentment (p. 341). Although on this earth the wicked may prosper, and the just be oppressed, the final reward of the just is in heaven. This must be the case if only to remedy the injustices of this world. But since the soul is immaterial, it can survive the body. Because soul and body are by nature so different, their union is a violent one, which, when it ceases, allows each substance to return to its natural condition. The soul regains all the force it had to employ in moving the passive and dead matter which is the body, so that the life of the soul really begins only with the death of the body (pp. 343–4). Since the identity of the self depends on the memory, and it is sufficient to be the same to remember having been, the continuity of one's existence after the death of the body will consist in our memory of our past existence. But, the Savoyard vicar claims, when the self is freed from the illusions produced by the body and the senses, and will be able without disturbance to enjoy the contemplation of the Supreme Being and the eternal truths, the beauty of this order will penetrate our souls, and being uniquely occupied in comparing what we have done with what we ought to have done, the voice of conscience will recover all its force, and it will be then that 'the pure voluptuousness which springs from self-contentment, and the bitter regret of having debased oneself will distinguish by inexhaustible sentiments the lot that each will have prepared for himself' (p. 345).

But Rousseau is concerned to assert not only the ultimate rewards of justice in heaven, but also that men are inclined by their natures towards justice and the love of the general order and the common interest. He believes that there is an innate principle of justice in each man's soul, on the basis of which, and despite other maxims to the contrary, we judge our own actions and those of others to be good or bad. This principle he calls conscience (p. 352). Conscience is described as the voice of the soul, having the same relation to the soul as instinct to the body (p. 348). It is said to be the infallible judge of good and evil and a certain guide for men (p. 354). It is the idea of conscience which provides the justification for Rousseau's statement that 'everything I feel to be good is good, everything I feel to be evil is evil' (p. 348). But while these descriptions of conscience suggest that it is through conscience that we have knowledge of good and evil, the Savoyard vicar also says that we are dependent on reason for the identification of the good, and that the role of conscience is to make us love it, which reason cannot do for us (p. 354). Conscience is here described as a sentiment. These statements are compatible with each other only if we say that the identification of the good through reason on which the awakening of conscience is dependent, is not so much a continuing process of judging what is good in this or that circumstance, but is a once-and-for-all development or reorientation of the individual towards a different conception of what is the good for him, a conception of his relation to the moral order, to which he is then held by the voice of conscience infallibly telling him when he is or is not living up to this new conception. This view would fit the account Rousseau gives of the transformation of Emile that is attendant upon his acquiring a social and moral consciousness. On this view, while reason is important in the initial identification of the moral order, it is ultimately sentiment or conscience that commits us to it. Reason by itself is powerless to combat the forces that incline us to evil.

In the above account evil is identified with subjection to the senses or the passions, so that one acts according to the impulsion of external objects. The Savoyard vicar also says that it consists in listening to what nature tells our senses rather than our hearts, and involves the subjection of the active principle in man to the commands of the passive (p. 348). How it is possible for the active principle to become subject to the passive he explains only very briefly by saying that through the union of soul and body, the soul acquires a concern for the preservation of the body, which inclines it to give preference to itself, contrary to the general order; nevertheless, the soul is capable of perceiving and loving the general order at the same time (p. 357). Why there should be this union, which obstructs the soul's attainment of the good, Rousseau does not know, but as a consequence of it he aspires

to the moment when, liberated from the fetters of the body, I will be *myself* without contradiction, without division, I will have need only of myself to be happy; meanwhile I am already in this life, for I count for little all evils, which I consider as almost foreign to my being, and because all the true good that I can obtain depends on me. (p. 358)

The importance of this argument concerning the dual nature of the self as composed of two opposed substances, soul and body, is that it establishes a radical contradiction within the self between two modes of its being, with the result that the good human life on earth is conceived of as a perpetual struggle of the self against itself in order to maintain the supremacy of the soul over the body. To find at this point in Rousseau's writings this conception of the self and of the nature of good and evil is surprising for three reasons. In the first place it is surprising to find a contradiction within human nature at all. For at the beginning of *Emile* Rousseau speaks with contempt of the bourgeois who is always torn between his duty and his inclinations, and opposes to the bourgeois the idea of a man, either natural man or the citizen, who is always at one with himself. And what he proposes in reconciling nature and society is to remove the contradictions in man (pp. 10–11). But now we have a fundamental contradiction asserted as an integral part of human nature. Secondly, it is surprising to find the contradiction located within nature itself. For up to this point Rousseau has proceeded on the assumption that nature is wholly good and that the evil in man springs from what might or might not be contradictions between nature and society. But now we have the principle of evil identified in terms, not of the social corruption of man's nature, but of human nature itself without reference to society. Thirdly, as the whole programme of *Emile* is aimed at removing the contradictions in man by reconciling nature and society, the present identification of these contradictions as occurring in man himself, because of his dual nature, makes it appear that that programme was wholly misconceived.

These reasons for finding the argument of the profession of faith surprising are at the same time reasons for thinking that, in the course of developing his programme in *Emile*, Rousseau came to an implicit awareness that his argument could not achieve what it purported to be achieving, namely such a reconciliation between nature and society, man and citizen, that the new social man would always be at one with himself and others. For if we posit no such awareness it is impossible to understand how Rousseau could have any interest in presenting an argument which undermines the assumptions on which his programme is based. On the other hand we cannot assume an explicit recognition, for Rousseau again makes no acknowledgement of the difficulties for the general coherence of his whole position that the argument of the Savoyard vicar creates. For such an implicit or intuitive awareness to be a plausible assumption, it must of course be supported by considerations showing that the development of Rousseau's programme in *Emile* has not achieved what it set out to achieve. But this is what my analysis of Rousseau's argument in the last section claims. There I argued, firstly, that Rousseau's solution to his social problem left no way of dealing with conflicts of ends, for to achieve this it would be necessary to develop the spirit of compromise, which involves each being concerned for the particular identity and value he has for another; and secondly, that the desire for such a particular identity for others is, as is evident from Rousseau's own argument, deep-rooted in man, 'natural' to him in society. However, it is this desire that constitutes Rousseau's social problem, and the whole point of his solution is its elimination. Consequently, if it cannot be eliminated through the emergence of superior understanding of self and others because of its 'natural' roots, Rousseau's solution will involve a permanent contradiction within each man.

As the argument of the profession of faith posits a dual existence in man and a continuous struggle against oneself for the attainment of the higher existence, which at the same time can never be fully realized in an earthly condition, it gives some plausible support to my analysis in the last chapter of what Rousseau's position truly involves. For against the spirit and suppositions of his argument he introduces this contradiction and division within man at just the point at which his solution to the social problem should be producing the contrary result. My analysis makes sense of this by showing why Rousseau should feel the necessity to introduce some such account of a dual and contradictory human nature as we find in the profession of faith.

But why cannot he explain the tensions in man that his position creates in terms of social causes of evil in accordance with the argument of the *Discourse* and the suppositions of the early part of *Emile*? His difficulty here arises out of the fact that on the one hand he claims to have solved the social problem by reconciling nature and society and by showing how nature is fully realized in a proper social consciousness, and that on the other everything remains as before; the same conflict between duty and inclinations, love of the common interest and love of self-interest. He cannot now account for the evil in man in terms of the social corruption of a good human nature without admitting that he has solved nothing, for he has already posited the right social consciousness. The tensions that remain despite this new social consciousness must be explained on another principle. Furthermore, what he needs is an account of the nature of the self that lends support to the individual in his struggle against himself and aspiration to an ideal existence. The development of the required conception of the self involves an explanation in the same terms of what the self has to struggle against, and so the location of the principle of evil in man himself and not in society.

My claim is that the metaphysical and dualist conception of the self that Rousseau develops in the account of the Savoyard vicar reflects the split that occurs within the new man between his moral will and his 'natural' desire to be related to others as a particular. The vicar's idea of the self is the symbolic expression of an underlying conflict within the personality consequent upon the adoption by the individual of certain ideas of how he should be related to others. This claim must be justified.

The significance of the Savoyard vicar's account lies not in the distinction between mind and body, but in the relation he conceives to exist between them. Mind is essentially independent of the body in which it is only temporarily located as in a hostile medium. Mind is the self aspiring to an ideal existence consisting in the life of the moral will. The body is dissociated from the self. It is experienced as entirely alien to the self, or alien to the 'true' self, and so as some other self, a base or lower self, in contrast with the higher self of the mind. This real or higher self comes fully into existence only when it is liberated from the body and from the opposition which the body constitutes for it. According to my claim, body in the above account must symbolize the will for a particular existence for another, and mind must represent the will for the common good and common identity in abstraction from all particularity. The body does not symbolize particularity as such, since the particular will, provided it is a will for ends independent of others and in accordance with the common good, is acceptable to Rousseau. Thus also the body in so far as it is subject to and controlled by mind is acceptable. It is particular being, not for oneself alone, but for another, that is corrupting, and it is this that the body symbolizes. How does the body symbolize it? The body is the external manifestation of the self. It is through one's physical being that one appears to another and comes to have an existence for him. Hence concern for one's particular being for another is most naturally and immediately expressed in concern for one's physical appearances.

Since under Rousseau's new order one's relations to others are to be relations to abstract individuals, no differentiating particularity can be allowed to enter in. So the individual's body as essentially particularized must be removed from the relation. Appearing to another in a particular body is a direct impediment to a right relationship with him. Hence being for another requires dissociation from one's body. But this is not in itself a reason for treating the body as the source of evil and conflict. Inner withdrawal from the external appearances of the self would be sufficient. The body would be seen merely as alien and irrelevant. But if man has a strong desire for a particular existence for others, and if this desire is seen as corrupt, involving the wrong relation to another, then a violent inner conflict will ensue between this desire on the one hand and the need to suppress it for the sake of the right relation to others on the other hand. The body as the external manifestation of the particular self is the natural symbol both for this desire and for its evil.

This profound dissociation of the self from the body is further expressed in terms of the body's determination from outside as a passive thing, and the mind's free, self-determining existence as active. Here the body's determination from outside represents the determination of the individual's particular identity by the opinion of others resulting from his concern for this identity, while the mind's freedom, and the body's determination in accordance with mind, represents the individual's determining his own particular identity for himself without reference to others.

In saying that the body in the Savoyard vicar's metaphysics

symbolizes the will for a particular existence for others, I do not mean that Rousseau explicitly uses the body symbolically in this fashion. He uses it symbolically without full awareness because as I have argued above, the original source of evil, *amour-propre*, should by now have withered away and so cannot be approached directly, and yet he is aware that serious tensions will remain in the individual's relations with others. By claiming that the body is the symbolic expression of inner conflict, however, I am claiming that were the conflict to be removed, the experiences leading to the adoption of this particular type of mind–body dualism would disappear, and so also would the corresponding metaphysics. If the inner conflict is only the consequence of a false conception of the individual's relations to others, the metaphysics must be incoherent also.

The experience at the root of the argument is the individual's rejection of his body as a way of being for another, and his withdrawal from externality into an inner life, a life of being for himself alone. It is an attempt to represent this experience in terms of a relation between mind and body that produces, if not incoherence, at least some insoluble difficulties.

Thus mind and body are supposed to be essentially independent of each other, the mind self-activating, the body passively determined from outside. And yet mind can determine body and body mind. Rousseau admits this is incomprehensible, but is satisfied with the mystery. The mystery only arises because the self dissociates itself from the body, and treats the body as alien. But this experience of one's body is by no means necessary and seems to arise only because the body stands for externality, whereas it is external existence that one is withdrawing from.

Also the following sequence arises: in withdrawing from the body, the self treats the body as not-self, as alien. But this is incompatible with Rousseau's claim that the individual is responsible for the evil he does. For if the source of evil were the body and the body were an alien being, the self as mind could always withhold assent to the acts of the body and remain pure and uncorrupted. But if the self is responsible, and it is the body that is the source of the evil, the body must be owned in some way. Yet it has to be owned as a separate force from the active principle of mind. So it appears as a lower or base self in constant opposition to the higher or real self. What, then, is the relation between the two selves? There must be some further self or unity that owns both the warring selves, otherwise it could not be the same 'I' that both willed and did not will in constant struggle. But this further self is obviously the potential unity of the person, and the warring selves merely modes in which that person experiences himself. This experience also is by no means a necessary one, but rather the product of contradictory responses to the external life.

ALIENATION

According to my argument of this chapter Rousseau's project for the new man is a withdrawal from the external life into himself. I do not mean by this a withdrawal into physical isolation but a withdrawal from the consciousness of others into isolation in his own. However, in the final stages of the education of Emile Rousseau's concerns centre on the dangers of the sexual passion now become unavoidable and the need of Emile for a wife. He discusses the qualities and education of a woman suitable to become the wife of the hero, and in her pursuit takes Emile into Parisian society. Turning away from Parisian society, because not surprisingly she is not to be found in it, there succeeds a romantic story of her discovery in the country and the course of their true love. But in the search for her in society Rousseau takes the opportunity of describing Emile's behaviour in his relations with others, and while he turns out not to be the polished and sophisticated ideal of that society, nevertheless he is presented as agreeable and attentive in his manners in a way which does not suggest a man who has withdrawn into an inner isolation. And this supposed inner isolation of himself from others appears even more false when set beside Emile's love relation with his Sophie. For here he does not hold himself back from the relation but gives himself entirely to the beloved. Have I not then misunderstood Rousseau's project?

The inner withdrawal in my interpretation arose out of the moral necessity to make oneself independent of the opinions and judgements of others, and so involved the refusal to allow oneself to appear to be judged by others in one's relations. The inner with-

drawal was a detachment of oneself from one's external appearances
for others. Now we find Emile in Parisian society having the desire
to make himself agreeable and to please others. Rousseau comments
thus:

Although the desire to please no longer leaves him absolutely indifferent
to the opinion of others, he will take from this opinion only what relates
immediately to his person, without attending to those arbitrary apprecia-
tions whose only law is fashion or prejudice. He will have pride enough
to want to do well all that he does, even to want to do it better than another:
he will wish to be the fastest in running, the strongest in wrestling, the most
skilful in work and the most clever at games of skill; but he will seek little
the advantages that are not clear in themselves, and which need to be
established by the judgement of others, as having more intellect than
another, as speaking better, as being more knowledgeable etc. . . . (p. 423)

Emile then is in some sense content to appear to others, but the
important point is that he is content to appear in activities in which
his performances will be clear in themselves and will not need
human judgement to establish his achievement. Where performances
in an activity do not have this clarity in themselves, but depend for
their assessment on human judgement, whether his own or others,
he is not interested. But in respect of one activity falling into this
latter category, namely his moral performances, Rousseau has this
to say:

Loving men because they are his fellows, he will love above all those who
are most like him, because he will feel himself to be good; and judging
of this resemblance by the conformity of taste in moral matters, in all that
concerns a good character, he will be very content to be approved. He will
not say exactly: I am glad because I am approved of; but I am glad because
men approve of the good that I have done: I am glad because those who
honour me do themselves honour; so long as they continue to judge so
soundly, it will be a fine thing to obtain their esteem. (p. 423)

Here the difficulty arising out of one's moral activity not being, like
running or wrestling, clear in itself, but dependent on human judgement for its assessment, and thus open to the judgement of others, is
avoided by Emile's certainty that his self-judgement and self-
assessment are correct. He is content to appear to and be approved
by others in so far as he attends only to those judgements which

conform to his own. His appearances for others are governed by the requirement that he pay no attention to their judgements of his performances as independent and possibly superior judgements to his own. In the one case this is because no judgements are required, he has won the race or the game, although it is a very limited view of the human interest in such activities to suppose it restricted to the question as to who has won and lost, and not to include the qualities displayed in the winning and the losing, things not clear in themselves. In the other case it is because he treats the judgements of others as merely reflexions of his own, doing honour primarily to them and not to him, for he is secure. His appearances for others can make no difference to his own self-conception, for he does not engage his own identity for himself in these appearances. He has got to hold to the position in which how he appears to others means effectively nothing for him. Or rather, in so far as others may be important for him, it will be as backing for himself, as extensions of his own judgement, and not as separate persons. Others will be important only as they reflect and support his own self-conception, so that they can be admitted only by being incorporated into his own identity for himself. In this sense he does not allow himself to appear to others at all, and it is this that constitutes the essential inner withdrawal and isolation of Rousseau's position. For he withdraws himself from any significance his particular being can have for others, not as himself or as extensions of himself, but as other than himself. He cannot attend to any such potential significance without attending to the judgements of others as separate and different from his own, where attending to means being prepared to allow such judgements to affect what he is for himself. By undertaking the project of being for himself in society, as in nature, independent of all such judgements, he isolates himself within his own consciousness and has to exist for himself alone.

There remains the question of the most personal relationship of all, Emile's love relation with his Sophie. Here at least it might be presumed that the inner isolation of the new man is broken down. It is, however, not so. In the first place Rousseau's conception of love is such that any real relation between two persons as lovers is unlikely to be established. Thus he says of love:

There is no true love without enthusiasm, and no enthusiasm without an object of perfection real or chimerical, but always existing in the imagination. What will set on fire lovers for whom this perfection is no longer anything, and who see in the person they love only the object of sensual pleasure? No, it is not thus that the soul becomes excited and gives itself up to those sublime transports which constitute the ecstasy of lovers and the charm of their passion. In love, everything is only illusion, I admit; but what is real is the love of true beauty that it creates in us. This beauty is not in the object one loves, it is the product of our illusions. But what does it matter? Does one the less sacrifice all these low sentiments to this imaginary mode? Is one's heart the less penetrated by the virtues with which one endows the person one cherishes? Does one detach oneself the less from the baseness of the human ego? Where is the true lover who is not ready to immolate his life to his mistress? And where is the sensual and gross passion in a man who wishes to die? (pp. 494–5)

Love, for Rousseau, is not a relation in which both lovers are present to each other in respect of their real qualities, but in respect of ideal qualities which they do not possess, but which it is necessary for each to attribute to the other for them to be capable of love at all. The lovers are present to each other as purely imaginary beings, and so themselves are not present at all. They do not mean anything to each other in terms of what they can really offer each other from the resources of their actual qualities. Their meaning for each other is what each creates for himself out of his own imagination. In this way the illusion of a personal relationship with another is created, the most dangerous because the closest of relationships, in which one exists wholly for the other, and in which the adaptation of each to the differentiated particularity of the other is most necessary, while its reality is successfully denied. The lover does not abandon his isolated consciousness, for the beloved has no substance, but is merely the creation of his own consciousness. He remains not exactly alone with himself, but alone with the imaginary being of his consciousness. There is no contact with a separate consciousness. The value of this love for the lover is the same as the value for the individual of his love of the moral good. The lover feels himself to be significantly related to another person without attending to that person's particularity, as the individual in his love of the moral good feels himself related to others but not as particulars. His self-exaltation in his love does not simply dispense him from paying, but requires him not to pay, attention to the particularity of his beloved, just as the individual's love of the moral good involved the denial of the relevance for him of the particularity of others. In this way he obtains the sense of a full existence of himself and a full relation to another which secures him at the same time from having to acknowledge the importance for himself of another consciousness than his own, and from having to accept that he exists for himself also in the consciousness of another.

The lover's attachment is not to a real person, and yet the imaginary being to which he attaches himself is identified with the spatial location of a real person. And the dependence that is thus created gives rise to dangers which are the occasion for the last moral teaching that Emile receives. After months of happiness with his Sophie, Emile, who is still under the direction of his tutor, is commanded to separate himself from her, in order to undertake travels for his further education and enlightenment. But an essential point is the separation itself. Emile must learn to be able to do without his Sophie, in order that his existence should not be committed to this relationship. The tutor explains himself to Emile thus:

When you entered upon the age of reason, I secured you from the opinion of men; when your heart became sensitive, I preserved you from the empire of the passions. If I could have prolonged this inner calm to the end of your life, I would have ensured the safety of my work, and you would have been as happy as a man can be; but, dear Emile, I steeped your soul in the Styx in vain, I have not been able to render it invulnerable everywhere; a new enemy has arisen, which you have not yet learnt to conquer and from which I have not been able to save you. This enemy is yourself. Nature and fortune had left you free. You could endure poverty; you could support the pains of the body, those of the soul were unknown to you; you depended on nothing but the human condition, and now you depend on all the attachments you have given yourself; in learning to desire, you have made yourself the slave of your desires. (p. 565)

The tutor goes on to say that it is our affection rather than our needs that cause our sufferings and that what is needed is the imposition of a law on the appetites of our hearts. Emile has up to now been good rather than virtuous, and the virtuous man is he who knows how to conquer his affections. In that way he follows his reason and

conscience, and is free in becoming master of himself. It is not that
one has to destroy the affections and the attachments they involve,
but that one has to become master of them rather than allow them to
become masters of oneself (pp. 566–8). The final peroration goes
thus:

> Do you then wish to live happy and wise, attach your heart only to the
> beauty that does not perish; let your condition limit your desires, let
> your duties go before your inclinations; extend the law of necessity to
> moral matters; learn to lose what can be taken from you; learn to aban-
> don everything when virtue commands, to raise yourself above events,
> to detach your heart without letting events rend it, to be courageous in
> adversity in order never to be miserable, to be firm in one's duty in order
> never to be criminal. Thus you will be happy in spite of the accidents of
> fortune, and wise in spite of passions. Thus you will find even in the
> possession of fragile goods a voluptuousness that nothing can disturb; you
> will possess them without their possessing you, and you will feel that man,
> from whom everything escapes, enjoys only what he knows how to lose.
> (p. 569)

It is clear, then, that Emile is to have relations of affection with and
attachment to others and a human world, but he has at the same time
to achieve a certain sort of detachment from these relations. He has
to preserve himself from engaging himself in the relation in such a
way as to open himself to being deeply affected and disturbed by
what happens in them. The only way in which it is possible both to
have relations and yet to detach oneself from them is by not allowing
one's identity for oneself to be engaged in them, by not allowing oneself to appear, so that whatever happens in the relation, one's own
self-conception and self-concern will not be affected. For in so far as
one commits oneself in the relation by allowing what one is for
oneself to be governed by what happens in it, then the loss or
corruption of the relation will necessarily bring about a change in the
way in which one exists for oneself. By committing one's existence
for oneself to the fortune of other persons and events, one cannot
raise oneself above these. One has staked one's existence on what is
mortal and destructible, and one must take one's chance.

But in so far as one achieves this detachment of oneself from the
relations one has with others and with a human world, it would
seem that the relations can mean nothing to one, so that they could

hardly be relations of affection or attachment, and one could not enjoy them at all, whereas Rousseau is saying that it is in this detachment that one enjoys them most securely and voluptuously. How is this possible? It is just because one has detached oneself from the human world and is secure in one's own self-conception, that one can enter into relations in a human world, knowing that whatever happens one cannot be defeated or brought low by them. By withdrawing into oneself one is essentially dependent only on oneself, and one can enjoy the goods of the human world in the knowledge that they have no hold over one. But still what enjoyment is to be found, if oneself is not engaged? The goods of the human world must surely be matters of indifference, not of voluptuous pleasure? The point is, however, that one possesses them and is not possessed. The enjoyment is in this sort of possession. The enjoyment consists in having things and persons dependent on one and subject to one's control without oneself being dependent on them in return. The possession, as all possession, adds to the sense of one's own existence, but whereas in the normal case this possession involves a corresponding dependence of oneself on what is possessed, because one's identity is engaged, in the Rousseauan sort of possession there is no correspondence. The possession adds to one's sense of existence, but is pure superfluity and hence voluptuous in its quality, because it is an addition to what is by itself, one's identity, felt as impregnably secure. There is no commitment of oneself to what one makes one's own, no external dependence and so no danger to oneself.

But this form of possession, however mildly pursued, is nevertheless another form of personal imperialism. For it involves the attempt to appropriate the world and others without offering anything in return. In respect of human relations it requires the dependence of the other, the commitment of the other to oneself, but not one's own to the other. For in so far as both attempt to play the same game, there will be nothing for either to enjoy, the mere façade of a human relationship, in which each keeps himself securely apart. And a world of such men would be a barely human world, the mere empty shell of such a world, in which each, in trying to guard the treasured possession of his independent and purely self-determined identity, is left guarding an empty chamber and a vacuous self.

4

THE PRINCIPLES OF POLITICAL RIGHT

My primary aim in this chapter is to show that the character of the common good solution to the social problem which I posited in my analysis of *Emile* is made more or less explicit in the *Social Contract*, and to show more fully the incoherence of this solution. To do this, however, I must proceed by an analysis of the essential argument of the *Social Contract*.

This twofold aim assumes that the argument of the *Social Contract* is intended as a solution to the same problem as is the argument of *Emile*, and that the solution is essentially in the same terms in both works. In the case of the *Social Contract* it is given more precision and development by being worked out explicitly in the context of a limited community of persons. That the argument of the *Social Contract* aims at a solution to the same problem as that of *Emile* seems evident from the definition of that problem in the opening of *Emile* in terms of the contradictory claims of being a man and being a citizen, and from the declared aim as being the reconciliation of the two. Also that work concludes with an injunction to Emile to become a citizen, or, if this is nowhere possible at least to serve his country (*Emile*, p. 605), and contains a brief instruction for Emile in the duties of citizenship consisting of a summary of the principles of the *Social Contract* (*Emile*, pp. 584ff.). That the solution in the *Social Contract* is essentially in the same terms as in *Emile* will be established if the arguments of this and the last chapter are more or less correct.

The *Social Contract* is subtitled the *Principles of Political Right* and in so far as it contains such principles we ought to be able to discuss them without reference to any particular political condition, in reference rather to politics in general. However, it is often held that Rousseau's political principles are meant only to apply to a small city state. It is difficult to see what is meant by this. Offered as principles of political right they must be held to be applicable to any political régime as constituting the terms in which the legitimacy of political régimes are judged. It may be the case that small city states constitute those conditions in which the principles are most likely to be realized, but this is not to say that the principles are designed only to apply to such conditions. And if it is said that the realization of the principles in city state conditions appears as some Utopian vision of the good society, it is still necessary to distinguish the principles from the Utopia. If what we have are genuine principles for judging the political relations of men, then we must be able to discuss these separately from some Utopian conception of their realization.

I take the principles of political right, then, that Rousseau offers us in the *Social Contract*, to be intended to have general application in the sphere of politics, even if the consequence is general criticism and condemnation. This is what Rousseau himself seems to mean by the opening declaration of the work to the effect that his purpose 'is to consider if, in political society, there can be any legitimate and sure principle of government, taking men as they are and laws as they might be'.[1] If the principle is to govern men's political relations, taking men as they are, and not as they might conceivably be, Rousseau's aim cannot simply be to construct a very special case of dubious relevance to the understanding of political right in general. Furthermore he continues his opening remarks with the statement that he will try 'always to bring together what right permits with what interest prescribes so that justice and utility are in no way divided' (p. 23). The principles of political right must be such that they are fully compatible with the interests of those whose political relations they are intended to govern. The intention at least is to achieve such a compatibility, and not to present principles that political men might or might not have any interest in endorsing. Proceeding on the assumption, then, that Rousseau is offering us some general political principles and not simply a particular ideal vision, I shall consider these principles as far as possible apart from the specific arrangements to which Rousseau relates them.

[1] *The Political Writings of Rousseau*, ed. C. E. Vaughan, vol. II, p. 23. Unless otherwise stated all further page references in this chapter are to the *Social Contract* in vol. II of this edition. The translations in this chapter are those of Maurice Cranston, *The Social Contract*, Penguin Classics, 1968, reprinted by permission of A. D. Peters & Co.

Rousseau tells us that man was born free and that he is everywhere in chains. The freedom is of nature and the chains of society. Rousseau's aim, however, is not to show how the chains can be abolished and natural freedom recovered in society, for political society requires constraints and natural freedom consists in the absence of all such constraints. His aim is rather to show how the necessary constraints of political society can be legitimate and thereby compatible with, if not natural freedom, then an essential human freedom nevertheless. If there are to be constraints and if at the same time these constraints are to be legitimate, they involve right, even, Rousseau says, a sacred right serving as the basis of all other rights. This right is not a natural right, nor can it arise out of force, but must be founded on covenants. Thus the problem of political right is initially resolved into a question about the nature of the covenants on which the legitimacy of the political order is based (pp. 23–4). Because the problem is introduced in this way we are immediately returned to the state of nature argument of the *Discourse* and of traditional political philosophy. For the covenants that are to render a political order legitimate are covenants made by men in a condition of freedom and equality, and thus by men assumed to be in a state of nature.

In the *Discourse* the idea of the state of nature was used to show that the need for political order could not arise out of the original natural condition of mankind, but only out of nature already transformed by primitive social organization, out of the disorders consequent upon the social corruption of human nature and the growth of inequality in society. The covenant that Rousseau posited in that work as the basis of political order was proposed and made by men who were not properly in a state of nature and who were certainly not in a condition of freedom and equality. The covenanters were unequal in respect of position and possessions, so that the equality of rights presupposed by the covenant merely legitimized and guaranteed the unequal positions acquired prior to the formation of a strictly political society. It provided security for the rich and the superior and offered little or nothing, a purely formal and supposedly empty equality, to the poor and dispossessed. If the covenant is to be genuine and legitimate it would seem that the equality of rights must comprise more than this formal equality. In the *Social Contract*, however, we do not find Rousseau returning to the account in the *Discourse* and telling us how this genuine and legitimate covenant is to be arrived at from the same position. We find him simply assuming that the disorders arising in the state of nature have become such that it is necessary for men to create a political society in order to survive, without providing any explanation of what these disorders are or how they have arisen (p. 32). He can thus merely assume that the men making such a covenant are in a position of freedom and equality, without attending to the difficulties arising if they were not.

If the condition of a legitimate covenant is one made by men in a free and equal position, why should this be so? Because, according to Rousseau, men are born, or are by nature, free and equal, and force making no right, constraints can only be legitimate if they receive the free and equal consent of all those subject to them. The assertion that men are born free and equal does not involve the denial that men are born subject to paternal authority, but the claim that this subjection lasts only as long as the child is in need of his father's protection; once it is no longer necessary, the child is left his own master and independent, in respect of authority, of all others (p. 24). The assertion of natural freedom and equality is not a claim that men are equal in all respects, in their faculties of mind and body, but is a claim that 'no man has any natural authority over his fellows' (p. 27). And the grounds for this claim lie in the assumptions contained in the term 'natural'. For by this is meant in a state of nature, in the absence of all social activity and social order. In the absence of these how could any man claim to exercise authority over any other? In virtue of what could he substantiate such a claim? Not in virtue of superior force, for while force can compel obedience it cannot create a right to the obedience on which authority depends (pp. 26–7). And if not force, then in a state of nature there is no other claim at all. If men are by nature free and equal in respect of all authority, their subjection to authoritative constraints can only be legitimate if these are consented to. But this consent can only be supposed to be given if the authority consented to is seen to be in their own interests, where interests are defined on the basis of the initial natural position of freedom and equality. If the initial position on the basis of which interests were calculated and consent given were otherwise, as in the unequal covenant of the *Discourse*, the authority created would be fraudulent, because consented to when natural equality had already been eroded. This covenant could not have been made in everyone's interest, if all had considered it on the basis of their natural equality.

The condition of a legitimate political order is then that it be covenanted by men from a position of freedom and equality. This looks as though it makes Rousseau's argument dependent upon the supposition that men were at some time or other in such a position and made a covenant, the terms of which will shortly be considered. But it is important to see how such a supposition might seem unnecessary, so rendering superfluous the argument that the actual historical position of men is one in which no inequality exists. The vital question is not what covenant men who were actually in the required position of freedom and equality did make in their own interests, but what covenant men would make in their own interests, supposing them to be in such a position. In so far as the position is not one of equality, it is necessary for them to abstract themselves from their actual positions of inequality, and consider what they could consent to, supposing themselves to be free and equal. It is necessary to make this abstraction and take a standpoint outside the historically determined inequalities, for otherwise, as in the covenant of the *Discourse*, what a man will consent to in his own interest will depend on what his particular historical and unequal position is, which will not be in accordance with his natural position. But in this way whether or not we suppose an actual state of nature and an actual covenant, what is required is the assumption of a natural position of men in respect of authority, which is a position of equal freedom. The meaning that is given to this notion in Rousseau as in his predecessors is that of a state of nature. And it is the covenant that men in such a position would make with each other to create political order and authority that we are to consider as the basis of political right.

When men have arrived at a point in the state of nature where it is necessary for them to unite to preserve themselves from the disorders of this state, the problem is how they are to unite their forces so that their 'powers are directed by a single motive and act in concert' (p. 32) without endangering their own legitimate self-interest. This difficulty Rousseau formulates thus: 'How to find a form of association which will defend the person and goods of each member with the collective force of all, and under which each individual, while uniting himself with the others, obeys no one but himself and remains as free as before' (p. 32). This, Rousseau says, is the fundamental problem to which the covenant provides the solution. The freedom they possessed before was the natural freedom of the state of nature, and we have already been told that this freedom cannot be retained in political society. But in so far as they are to remain as free as they were before, the essence of that freedom must remain even if the form in which it is enjoyed has to change. Natural freedom consisted in the absence of all external human constraints, and was limited only by the physical power of the individual, but it also meant that the individual obeyed no one but himself, was his own master, and depended on the authority of no other man. It is this being one's own master and obeying no one but oneself that is specifically stated by Rousseau as a necessary condition of a satisfactory political association. But it obviously cannot be enjoyed in the same way as in the state of nature. If its essence is to remain, the way in which it is to be secured will have to be very different.

The articles of the contract which is to secure this result, Rousseau says, are precisely determined by the nature of the act, so that any modification nullifies it, and although Rousseau admits that they have perhaps never been formally acknowledged, he claims that they are everywhere the same and everywhere given tacit recognition. The violation of the contract involves the loss of the social freedom gained through it, but the recovery of the individual's natural freedom and original rights. What then are the necessary articles of the contract? These, Rousseau says, are reducible to a single one, 'namely the total alienation by each associate of himself and all his rights to the whole community' (p. 33). Rousseau says of this contract first that because each individual gives himself absolutely, the condition is the same for all, so that no one has an interest in making it onerous for others; secondly, that since the alienation is total, no individual has any rights to claim against the community. The advantage of this is that with no rights left to individuals, there cannot occur a conflict between the claims of the community on the one hand and the claims of individuals on the other, which could not be settled by reference to a higher authority. If individuals retain certain rights against the community, they will in these cases be judges in their own cause, and will soon demand to be such judges in all matters. The state of nature would remain, and the association become tyrannical or void. Finally, Rousseau claims that, since each alienates himself to all, as the whole community, he gives himself to no one. Each gains the same rights over others as others gain in respect of himself, so that each recovers what he has given up, and acquires furthermore more power to preserve what he has (p. 33).

The total alienation of oneself and all one's rights to the community must mean that one surrenders one's natural independence and self-direction, and accepts in its place the direction of oneself by the community. One's point of reference and interest ceases to be oneself and becomes the community. It is for this reason that no rights can be retained by the individual independent of the community, for the individual would then retain a point of reference and interest which would be himself apart from the community. He would not have become this fully communally orientated and directed person, but would be half this new person and half the old natural and independent self. He would be properly neither the one nor the other. In becoming this communal person and surrendering himself to community direction, the individual, Rousseau claims, gives himself to no one. But this must be false, unless the community cannot act without the concurrence of each individual, so that unanimous decisions are required and every man has his veto. If this were not so, one would have to say that each individual surrenders himself to all the rest, or to those who at any one time have the authoritative direction of the community in their hands. So to understand the immediate significance of the individual's surrender one must know how the authoritative direction of the community is to be determined. Of this Rousseau has to say that, eliminating all that is not essential to the contract, it can be reformulated thus:

'Each one of us puts into the community his person and all his powers under the supreme direction of the general will: and as a body, we incorporate every member as an indivisible part of the whole' (p. 33). The authoritative direction of the community lies not with any part of the community, but with the general will. In surrendering oneself to the direction of the community, one is surrendering oneself to direction by the general will, so that the general will has got to be such that in giving oneself to it, one is giving oneself to no one, and through obeying the general will, one must be obeying no one but oneself and remain as free as before. The general will, if it does not actually involve unanimous decisions and give to every man a veto, as it does not and clearly could not sensibly do, must nevertheless, to deliver the required goods, produce essentially the same effects.

This act of association, Rousseau says, immediately replaces the individual person of each contracting party 'with an artificial and collective body composed of as many members as there are voters in the assembly' (p. 33), and gives to that body 'its unity, its common ego, its life and its will' (p. 33). The public person so formed, Rousseau calls a *republic* or *body politic*, which is said to be the *state* in its passive role, and the *sovereign* in its active role. Its members he collectively calls a *people*, individually in so far as they share in the sovereign power *citizens*, and as they are subject to the laws of the state *subjects*. Each member has a dual status as both citizen and subject, and the contract involves a commitment of the individual in both respects, as a member of the sovereign body in relation to other citizens, as subject in relation to the sovereign. While as subject the individual is obliged by the acts of the sovereign, the sovereign itself cannot be limited by any prior act, but must be in relation to the affairs of the community absolute and unlimited. The sovereign is, according to Rousseau, in the position of a private person contracting with himself. It makes no more sense to suppose the sovereign to have restrictions imposed by law on its powers than it would in the case of the self-contracting private person.

However unlimited the sovereign necessarily is by law, this is, we are told, no cause for concern. The sovereign has no need to give guarantees to its subjects because 'by the mere fact that it is, [it] is always all that it ought to be' (p. 35). Being composed of all the members of the community its interests must be the same as theirs, and on the one hand it is absurd to suppose that it could wish to hurt all its members at the same time, and on the other it cannot while remaining what it is – the sovereign – distinguish any particular member adversely. Why this last condition is so will have to be seen, but at any rate in the present formulation, subjection to the sovereign, the community in its active role directing itself through the general will, involves not only giving oneself to no one, and obeying oneself alone, but a condition in which one's interests cannot be harmed.

The transformation from the state of nature to civil or political society involves for Rousseau a radical change in man from the rule of instinct to the rule of morality, from physical impulse to duty and from inclinations to reason. What man loses is his natural liberty. What he gains is in the first place civil liberty, or his freedom within the law, and secondly secure property rights instead of mere possession. But he also acquires moral freedom, 'which alone makes man master of himself' (p. 37), and is brought about by 'obedience to a law one prescribes to oneself' (p. 37). Finally, he gains equality. What at this point Rousseau has briefly to say about equality is what he also says could serve as a basis for the whole social system.

Namely, that the social pact, far from destroying natural equality, substitutes, on the contrary, a moral and lawful equality for whatever physical inequality that nature may have imposed on mankind; so that however unequal in strength and intelligence, men become equal by covenant and by right. (p. 39)

All these goods brought about by the creation of legitimate political society and dependent upon the total alienation of each individual to the community, require that the community be directed by the general will alone, and so to understand how they are secured, it is necessary to begin a consideration of what this general will is.

The general will is to be expressed in laws promulgated by a general assembly composed of all adult men of the community, at which decisions are to be made by some form of majority vote. This assembly possesses the legislative authority in the community, and the individual as subject is subject to this authority. Legislative authority is what Rousseau calls sovereignty, the supreme authority in the community. But this sovereignty pertains to decisions of the general assembly not simply as such, but only in so far as they are expressions of the general will, and the individual is obliged to obey only on this condition. Since a majority vote of the general assembly may not be an expression of the general will, what is needed is a characterization of the general will which will enable us to distinguish between decisions of a general assembly which are, and ones which are not, expressions of the general will.

The general will, Rousseau says, is the will a man has as a citizen, and is to be distinguished from the private will he has simply as a man. The general will is here referred to as involving the public interest, while the private will involves private interest (p. 35). Later the general will is said to be directed at the common good (p. 39) or public good (p. 42). The terms public interest, public good, common interest and common good are used interchangeably by Rousseau, and the central distinction here is quite clear. There is on the one hand the citizen's will for the common good, which is the general will, and on the other the individual's will for private interest. These two tend naturally to conflict, for 'the private will inclines by its very nature towards partiality, and the general will towards equality' (p. 40).

The crucial question becomes the nature of the common good, which is the object of the citizen's general will, and its relation to private interest. Rousseau says:

if conflict between private interests has made the setting up of civil societies necessary, harmony between those same interests has made it possible It is what is common to those different interests which yields the social bond; if there were no point on which separate interests coincided, then society could not conceivably exist. And it is precisely on the basis of this common interest that society must be governed. (pp. 39–40)

We have then, in the first instance, different private interests. The common good or common interest is what these different private interests have in common. If each individual seeks security for the pursuit of his own ends, then however much private ends may differ, each has the same interest in the security to pursue them.

Rousseau distinguishes the general will from what he calls the will of all. The former, he says, 'studies only the common interest, while the will of all studies private interest, and is indeed no more than the sum of individual desires' (p. 42). While it is not at all clear what sort of sum this will of all is, he goes on to say that if we take away from the individual desires 'the pluses and minuses that cancel each other out, the sum of the difference is the general will' (p. 42). And this sum seems equally unclear. He has, however, a footnote to this statement which begins with a quotation from the Marquis d'Argenson:

'Every interest has its different principles. Harmony between two interests is created by opposition to that of a third.' He might have added
the harmony of all interests is created by opposition to those of each. If
there were no different interests, we should hardly be conscious of a
common interest, as there would be no resistance to it; everything would
run easily of its own accord, and politics would cease to be an art. (p. 42,
note 2)

The common interest, Rousseau seems to be saying, is created by opposition to the private interest of each. For this to be true private interest would have to be defined as a selfish interest, such that by opposing this selfishness in each a non-selfish common interest is achieved.

If we apply this to the statement to which it is supposed to be an explanatory footnote, about pluses and minuses cancelling each other out, the result would seem to be this. Each begins by expressing his private interest, which is his selfish desire for an arrangement for the community designed to give him as an individual an advantage over all others. By cancelling out the selfish element in the arrangements each proposes, we are left with an arrangement which gives no one the preference but treats all equally. For example, suppose that a collection of individuals in a situation of conflict regulated by no rules are debating what arrangements might be introduced to in-crease their individual security. Each begins by proposing a rule which will be to his maximum private advantage. The character such a rule will have for each is that of restrictions being imposed on the behaviour of all others but excluding himself. Provided all agree on the same restrictions that are to be imposed on others, but disagree only in respect of those to whom the restrictions are to apply, then cancelling out all the selfish elements, i.e. the self-exemptions from the operation of the rule, will leave, as the common element in every individual's desire, the same rule now applying to all.

The general will would appear to be from this a sort of equality defined in opposition to the selfish partiality of the private will. We have already seen that the general will and the private will are said to tend in opposite directions, to equality on the one hand and partiality on the other. This opposition seems now to be not so much a tendency as of the very essence of each.

The immediate question, however, is what sort of equality is involved in the general will. Rousseau says of the general will and its connexion with equality this:

The commitments which bind us to the social body are obligatory because they are mutual; and their nature is such that in fulfilling them a man cannot work for others without at the same time working for himself. How should it be that the general will is always rightful and that all men constantly wish the happiness of each but for the fact that there is no one who does not take that word 'each' to pertain to himself and in voting for all think of himself? This proves that the equality of rights and the notion of justice which it produces derive from the predilection which each man has for himself and hence from human nature as such. (p. 44)

In this passage the equality required is an equality of rights. This is presented as the condition under which voting has to be carried on. Whatever is voted must satisfy the condition that it provides equal rights for all. This ensures that nobody can obtain a preferential advantage for himself over others. Nobody can legitimately desire for himself anything without desiring it for others also, or obtain rights for others without securing them for himself. Thus it appears that each in working for himself is working for others, and in working for others works for himself.

However, the continuation of the above passage begins to obscure the clarity and simplicity of this understanding of equality. It goes thus:

It also proves that the general will, to be truly what it is, must be general in its purpose as well as in its nature; that it should spring from all and apply to all; and that it loses its natural rectitude when it is directed towards any particular and circumscribed object – for in judging what is foreign to us, we have no sound principle of equity to guide us. (p. 44)

This passage introduces two further considerations, generality and universality. It is specifically stated that generality is required, and he goes on to elucidate the requirement that the object of the general will be not particular and circumscribed as the opposite of generality. Universality is specified in so far as it is stated that the general will must apply to all. These three considerations are not the same, yet it seems that Rousseau is supposing that they are. Equality (equal rights) is not the same as universality (applying to all), since a rule or law can apply to all and yet grant unequal rights. Nor is universality the same as generality, since a rule or law can be general, that is, specify no individuals by name, but only general properties or characteristics, without applying to all.

The question arises immediately as to whether Rousseau intends to specify three separate conditions that have to be satisfied for something to count as a genuine expression of the general will, or whether he is supposing that he is specifying one condition only. I think it will become clear that he confuses systematically these three conditions. He moves from one to the other supposing all the time that he is always using the same condition.

Rousseau stated in the above passage that the general will cannot consider a particular or circumscribed object. What Rousseau means by this he explains thus:

Whenever we are dealing with a particular fact or right, on a matter which has not been settled by an earlier and general agreement, that question becomes contentious. It is a conflict in which private interests are ranged on one side and the public interest on the other; and I can see neither the law which is to be followed nor the judge who is to arbitrate. It would be absurd in such a dispute to seek an express decision of the general will; for a decision could only be a conclusion in favour of one of the contending parties, and it would be regarded by the other party as an alien, partial will, a will prone to error and liable in such circumstances to fall into injustice. So we see that even as a private will cannot represent the general will, so too the general will changes its nature if it seeks to deal with an individual case; it cannot as a *general* will give a ruling concerning any one man or any one fact. (pp. 44–5)

The conclusion to this passage is explicitly the generality condition only. Yet in working up to this conclusion Rousseau thinks he is excluding the possibility of the general will being expressed in respect of issues where the particular interests of different individuals conflict. But the generality condition does not involve this exclusion. It excludes only decisions respecting the conflicting interests of particular individuals, but not decisions respecting the conflicting interests of general classes of persons.

From the above conclusion Rousseau returns immediately to the equal rights condition thus:

It should nevertheless be clear from what I have so far said that the general will derives its generality less from the number of voices than from the common interest which unites them – for the general will is an institution in which each necessarily submits himself to the same conditions which he imposes on others; this admirable harmony of interest and justice gives to social deliberations a quality of equity which disappears at once from the discussion of any individual dispute precisely because in these latter cases there is no common interest to unite and identify the decision of the judge with that of the contending parties. (p. 45)

In this passage the generality condition is explicitly identified with the equal rights condition. Furthermore he assumes that anything which satisfies the equal rights condition will be a common interest.

From here we move rapidly to the desired conclusion respecting freedom. First, a resounding reaffirmation of the equal rights condition:

Whichever way we look at it, we always return to the same conclusion: namely, that the social pact establishes equality among the citizens in that they all pledge themselves under the same conditions and must all enjoy the same rights Hence by the nature of the compact, every act of sovereignty, that is every authentic act of the general will, binds or favours all citizens equally, so that the sovereign recognizes only the whole body of the nation and makes no distinction between any of the members who compose it. (p. 45)

Since Rousseau assumes that the equal rights condition ensures that a common interest will always be secured, then each need only will a law in his own interest under these conditions, and in doing so he wills the interest of all others at the same time. Thus Rousseau says 'so long as the subjects submit to such covenants alone, they obey nobody but their own will' (p. 45).

We have already arrived at the desired conclusion as to how each is, in subordinating himself to the community, to obey only himself and remain as free as in nature. Yet how the conclusion is arrived at should still be obscure. The central problem is this: how does the equal rights condition ensure that a common interest is always involved? It may be suspected that the derivation of common interests from the equal rights condition has something to do with Rousseau's systematic confusion between the equal rights condition, generality and universality.

So far, however, there seems little doubt that an equality of rights is required for an expression of the general will. But this apparent clarity also disappears when Rousseau proceeds to an elucidation of the nature of law.[1] In this chapter we find first of all the recurrence of the confusion between equality and generality, but this time with the addition of universality. He begins by repeating that the general will cannot relate to any particular object. But he immediately identifies this with the requirement of universality, thus:

I have already said that the general will cannot relate to any particular object. For such a particular object is either within the state or outside the state. If it is outside, then a will which is alien to it is not general with regard to it; if the object is within the state, it forms a part of the state. (p. 49)

And, he goes on to say, a part is less than the whole so that what does not satisfy the condition of generality does not apply to all. By implication what does satisfy the condition of generality applies to all (universality).

This identification of generality with universality is immediately extended to include one previous formulation of the equal rights condition, namely that there must be no distinctions whatsoever between one member of the community and another. The passage goes thus:

But when the people as a whole makes rules for the people as a whole, it is dealing only with itself; and if any relationship emerges, it is between the entire body seen from one perspective and the same entire body seen from another, without any division whatever. Here the matter concerning which

[1] Law for Rousseau is not simply a rule enacted by the general assembly, but is always an authentic act of the general will.

a rule is made is as general as the will which makes it. And *this* is the kind of act which I call a law. (p. 49)

But at this point he immediately proceeds to contradict the equal rights condition, thus:

When I say that the province of law is always general, I mean that the law considers all subjects collectively and all actions in the abstract; it does not consider any individual man or any specific action. Thus the law may well lay down that there shall be privileges. The law may establish several classes of citizens and even specify the qualifications which shall give access to those several classes, but it may not say that this man or that shall be admitted; the law may set up a royal government and an heredi-tary succession, but it may not elect a king or choose a royal family – in a word no function which deals with the individual falls within the province of the legislative power. (p. 49)

If the law can establish privileges and create several classes of citizens specifying the qualities giving membership of the various classes, it is clear that inequalities of a substantial nature can be created between citizens by authentic acts of the general will. The objection is not to the legal enactment of such inequalities but to the nomination of individual persons as beneficiaries. But if the law can create inequalities, then these can be just or unjust. Obviously Rousseau is supposing that the universality condition is also satisfied so that although we have a law granting unequal rights to different categories of person, the law must still be binding on all members of the community. No individuals can be exempted from its application. But even though both the generality and the universality conditions are satisfied, the inequalities created can still be unjust. For example a law which makes the burden of taxation fall more heavily on those least able to pay would seem unjust. However, such a law need name no individuals, but establish only categories of person, those with income above and below a certain amount. If the requirements of generality and universality are the only conditions for an enactment of the general assembly to count as an authentic act of the general will, then the general will can obviously be grossly unjust.

But Rousseau's clear specification of generality only[1] as the condi-tion of an authentic law and his clear admission of substantial in-

---

[1] Assuming universality to be included also.

equalities in no way distract him from his libertarian conclusion. The subsequent paragraph to the above passage returns to it. He says:

> On this analysis, it is immediately clear that we can no longer ask who is to make laws because laws are acts of the general will ... no longer ask if the law can be unjust, because no one is unjust to himself; and no longer ask how one can be both free and subject to the laws for the laws are but registers of what we ourselves desire. (pp. 49–50)

It was seen previously that the conclusion that everybody is only obeying himself depended on the presence of a common interest, and this seemed to depend on the satisfaction of the equal rights condition. Now that the equal rights condition is abandoned, or relaxed, at any rate contradicted, and only generality (even including universality) required, the presence of a common interest cannot be said to be a necessary condition for an authentic expression of the general will. But it is obvious that Rousseau is supposing that generality and universality ensure the presence of a common interest, and that this is sufficient to bring about the justice of the laws and the self-obedience of the subjects.

There is, then, much obscurity. But two things are clear. First, Rousseau systematically confuses equality (equal rights), generality and universality. Secondly, he believes that if certain conditions are met, though exactly which conditions these are constitutes the confusion, an interest common to all members of the community will necessarily be involved, and the presence of this common interest will ensure the justice of the laws and freedom of the subjects.

Let us recapitulate. From the last passage quoted it was clear that Rousseau supposed that generality was the same thing as universality and that while universality permitted unequal rights, it nevertheless ensured an equality in some sense which guaranteed the presence of a common interest. To begin, then, with the sole condition of generality and to formulate Rousseau's position: when a number of individuals are debating what rules to enact to govern their life together, provided that whatever is proposed satisfies the condition of generality, it will always involve a common interest. Each individual will be concerned to think of a rule which will protect his own interest, but since the conditions prevent him from distinguishing his interest qua separate individual, he can only propose a rule in his interest in so far as he generalizes that interest. Now Rousseau supposes that, given these conditions, no one will be able to separate off his interest, and so distinguish it from the interest of all other members of the community. Each in having to generalize his interest will have to think of an interest common to all, and thus arrive at a common interest.

However, in the conditions posited, it would be perfectly possible for individuals to think of a rule in their own interest where the interest served by the rule is generalized, but is still not common to all; that is when the rule proposed establishes favoured treatment for a class of persons, of which the individual is a member. Here the rule does not distinguish the individual's interest qua pure individual, but nevertheless distinguishes it from the interests of some other members of the community in terms of that individual's membership in a class.

Of this Rousseau is aware, for he recognizes that groups or sectional associations within the society can create a common interest of the group's members which will not be the common interest of all. But he concludes from this that such groups should not be permitted to exist (pp. 42–3). What he supposes, then, is that, if all groups and sectional associations are abolished, it will be the case that to generalize one's interest is to arrive at an interest common to all. But even here it is necessary to suppose that the abolition of groups and sectional associations involves the splitting up of the common interests that the groups embody into separate individual interests, so that to rise above these to any degree of generality is to arrive at what is common to all. However, since the groups and sectional associations are only organizations of underlying interests, the abolition of their organization cannot of itself abolish sectional or class interests, but only make it more difficult for what is common to them to be expressed. This difficulty is further increased by Rousseau's stipulation that the members of society should have 'no communication among themselves' (p. 42), by which presumably he means no political communication, no discussion of interests that some may share, outside the legislative assembly.

These measures are designed to ensure that the individual in respect of the interests he is aware of and pursues is on his own, that he is not allied or connected with a class or group of interests within the wider community. Thus if each thinks only of his independent individual interest as the interest of his that has to be secured by a general rule, then he can only secure it by identifying it as the interest of an abstract individual, an individual who is defined by his pursuit of ends but not by his pursuit of any particular ends. He thus arrives at an interest of his as abstract or pure individual that is necessarily the same for all other members of the community as such individuals, and so at a common interest.

In this way the requirement of generality, together with the isolation of the individual brought about by the suppression of groups and of political discussion outside the legislative assembly,[1] ensures that the universality condition will be met. At the same time a basic equality of rights will be secured for all as individuals, since the rights that each demands for himself as pure individual will always be the same as the rights that everyone else demands for himself. At this level there can be no conflicts of interest, but on the contrary each in working for himself will necessarily be working for others, and in working for others will necessarily be working for himself. Hence each, in subjecting himself to the community direction as expressed in the general will, is nevertheless only subjecting himself to what is his own interest as pure individual, and so in obeying the general will is obeying only himself and is as free as he was in nature.

But what about the inequalities and privileges that Rousseau says the general will may establish by law provided that the law does not designate particular individuals as beneficiaries? Such inequalities will be compatible with the fundamental equality of rights for all as pure individuals if they can be shown to be necessary for the better security of these rights. Thus Rousseau believes that a government or body of magistrates is necessary to enforce the general will against backsliders, even though the general will is everybody's will, and that this body will constitute a particular group with special privileges within the community. As such a particular group it is a

[1] But apparently inside also; see p. 104.

danger to the general will, since it will generate a group interest of its own necessarily antagonistic to the general will. Its existence and privileges are nevertheless justified in terms of the security it provides for the equal rights of individuals. The inequalities still serve all members of the community as pure individuals equally, although some may gain superior positions in the community as officials and magistrates. Provided inequalities within a community are always derived from the need to secure or foster the fundamental equal rights of all as pure individuals, no division between citizens as pure individuals will be created. No one as pure individual will be burdened or favoured more than another, but every man will count equally with every other.

According to the above account of Rousseau's political theory, the object of politics must be to make each person as a particular individual stand on his own, and think of himself and his interest independently of all others. This is indeed what Rousseau says is the proper object of every political system:

If we enquire wherein lies precisely the greatest good of all, which ought to be the goal of every system of law, we shall find that it comes down to two main objects, freedom and equality: freedom because any individual dependence means that much strength withdrawn from the body of the state, and equality because freedom cannot survive without it. (p. 61)

He goes on to say in elaboration of this passage that he has already explained what civil freedom is. Civil freedom is the right of the individual to 'do what he pleases with such goods and such freedom as is left to him by these covenants' (p. 46), i.e. by laws which are the expression of the general will. But the individual's subjection to such laws is subjection only to himself as pure individual or to others only in so far as they possess the same abstract identity. It is not subjection to or dependence on others in their particularity. In respect of the individual's particularity he is free to do what he pleases, provided that what he does, does not injure others (p. 131, note 2).

Equality, Rousseau says, is necessary to maintain this independence of others. The equality he is talking about here is not the equal rights of all as abstract individuals, but equality of power and wealth. These, he says, need not be absolutely the same for all.

Unequal power, however, is permissible only if authorized by law, and unequal wealth should never be such that the rich can buy the poor, or the poor have to sell themselves. Each individual in respect of wealth should be able to maintain his independence, and another should have power over him not as a particular individual, but as an organ of the community's will. In being so subject to another, the individual is subject only to his own will. His independence as a particular individual is not threatened.

The relations that should exist between members of a community, Rousseau sums up thus:

> . . . their relations among themselves should be as limited, and relations with the entire body as extensive as possible, in order that each citizen shall be at the same time perfectly independent of all his fellow citizens and excessively dependent on the republic . . . (p. 63)

Again dependence on the republic or the entire body is not a threat to the individual's liberty, for dependence on the general will is a form of self-dependence. Even if the general will authorizes unequal classes of citizens as a result of which one finds oneself in a subordinate position to others, one does not thereby become dependent on them as particular individuals with their own particular system of ends, but on them as agents of the general will and so of one's own.

This account of Rousseau's political theory shows it to be substantially the same solution to his social problem of dependence as the one to be found in *Emile*. It serves as a solution by ensuring that individuals can be related to each other in a community without becoming dependent on each other as particular individuals with particular systems of ends. Each is dependent on the other fundamentally only in respect of his abstract individual interest which is identical for each, so that he is related to another as a mere duplication of himself and his own interest, or as a mere agent or organ of the common will. As a particular individual with his own system of ends, he pursues them for himself without regard to others, so long as his ends do not impinge on the ends of others. As a particular individual each can exist, as in nature, for himself alone. This solution preserves the essential principle of nature, oneness, in so far as it is never a multiplicity of potentially conflicting particular wills and ends that the individual is faced with, but either his own particular will alone independent of others, or his abstract individual will which is identical with the will of all other such individuals.

As with the solution in *Emile* the obvious defect consists in the very fact that is supposed to make it a satisfactory solution – its exclusion of all situations in which the particular ends of different persons impinge on each other. The solution requires the elimination of all such situations, for without their elimination one will have to recognize and come to terms with the particularity of others as impinging on one's own particularity. An acceptable resolution of such conflicts between ends must involve the desire in each individual for the achievement of an ordering of all the various particular interests which will be pleasing to each as a particular individual. Each must come to desire to be related to others as particular individuals, to exist for them in his particularity. This for Rousseau is the very essence of corruption. But such situations cannot be supposed to disappear merely because they are considered undesirable.[1]

There is, furthermore, a peculiarity in this account of Rousseau's political theory, in that it makes him out to be a radical liberal or individualist, whose primary object is the maximization of individual freedom and whose concern for equality is a necessary condition of this. But more often Rousseau is presented as an extreme collectivist or totalitarian destroyer of individual freedom. This other view is also justified, for Rousseau does not hold consistently to the above account of the common interest. He admits as the legitimate objectives of a system of law, besides the general ones, liberty and equality, special objectives consisting in the particular interests of a people. He says:

In short, apart from those principles which are common to all, each people has its own special reasons for ordering itself in a certain way and for having laws that are fitted to itself alone. Thus it was, in the past, that the Hebrews, and more recently the Arabs, took religion as their chief object, while the Athenians had literature, Carthage and Tyre trade, Rhodes seafaring, Sparta war, and Rome civic virtue. (p. 62)

[1] As noted before there exists the possibility of the perfectly competitive market solution to this problem. But it is not Rousseau's solution, nor is it in any way an acceptable account of the right relations between persons in the market. It is important to note also that centralized ordering or planning is not a solution to *this* problem. For it to be a solution the ordering of society would have to be by reference to ends that are the same for all. But *ex hypothesi* we are dealing with conflicting ends, not common ends.

All the items on this list do not seem to be of the same kind, but nevertheless the principle involved is clear: a people may have particular ends by reference to the attainment of which it may order the community. These particular ends must be conceived of as common interests, otherwise the community would be ordered, and individuals subordinated, by reference to the particular ends of a section of the community. But trade, literature, seafaring cannot be common interests in the same sense of common interest as was used before. The common interest or good as hitherto conceived was the interest of each individual abstracted from his particular ends and universalized. It was necessarily a common interest precisely because it involved no reference to particular ends. So a particular end cannot be a common interest in the same sense. Yet Rousseau in no way acknowledges, and seems to be not at all aware, of the shift in type of common interest that has occurred. He seems to suppose that whatever he has said about the common interest, as the abstract interest of each individual, applies also to the common interest as particular end.

In what sense can a particular end, such as trade, be a common interest? One might think of it as the particular interest of each individual. Each individual might happen to have as his particular end trade. However, even if all members of a community are engaged in trade or dependent for their livelihood on trade in some way, one cannot suppose that each has exactly the same interest in it. All may acknowledge the prosperity of trade as their interest, and yet disagree because of different interests as to what particular policies should be pursued to further this common aim. A policy that suits one section may not suit so well another. Where we are dealing with particular ends we are dealing with situations in which individuals' interests naturally impinge on and conflict with each other. And yet if some such interest as trade is to serve as the organizing principle of a community, by reference to which some individuals may be subject to others, it must satisfy Rousseau's conditions for the general will and freedom. But to do this, it must be the identical interest for each individual, so that the individual in obeying the general will for this particular policy furthering trade, is obeying only his own will for his own interest. The particular interest must be, to be admitted as a Rousseauan community's end, a simple unity, an interest for each which merely duplicates the interest of every other, and not a complex unity, in which many different interests are held together in harmony. Only thus can the individual avoid becoming dependent on the particularity of others. But this is an impossible condition for a particular interest to meet.

The consequence of this view of the common interest is that on the one hand it now becomes legitimate for the community to consider in its public affairs substantive particular ends, but that on the other hand such particular ends can only be admitted at all if they are claimed as the identical interest of each individual, and not in their natural diversity as ends over which men may be expected to differ. Hence the natural disagreement between men over particular ends will appear in the political forum as unnatural conflict, in which either all are pursuing their divisive sectional interests or some are doing so against the true common interest. Anybody who wishes to favour some particular end will have to proclaim this as the common end which each individual really wills for himself, and will have to treat disagreement with his view as the product of selfishness and corruption. Since there is no natural basis for agreement on particular ends, and since this view of the common interest presupposes such agreement, there would exist extreme pressure on all to conform to somebody's idea of the common interest in order to manufacture the natural unity that is not there.

It is clear that Rousseau attributes to political communities substantive particular ends, and it is from this source that the language Rousseau employs to stress the singleness of the community derives. The representation of the natural diversity of many persons associated together as one person, one body possessing one will (pp. 33–4), expresses the need in Rousseau's view for a singleness of purpose to be discovered in the community to correspond to the singleness that is naturally there in the individual. The picture he needs to present of the community is as in the following passage:

So long as several men joined together consider themselves a single body, they have only one will, which is directed to their common preservation and general well-being. Then all the animating forces of the state are vigorous and simple; its principles are clear and luminous; it has no incompatible or conflicting interests; the common good makes itself so manifestly evident that only common sense is needed to discern it. Peace, unity, equality are enemies of political sophistication. (p. 102)

And in the next paragraph he continues:

A state thus governed needs very few laws, and whenever there is need to promulgate new ones, that need is universally seen. The first man to propose such a law is only giving voice to what everyone already feels, and there is no question either of intrigues or eloquence to secure the enactment of what each has already resolved to do as soon as he is sure that all others will do likewise. (p. 103)

This happy state is, however, dependent on only common interests being consulted, and in so far as 'particular interests begin to make themselves felt and sectional societies begin to exert an influence over the greater society, the common interest becomes corrupted and meets opponents' (p. 103), contradictions and disputes arise, and the general will ceases to receive expression in the laws of the community.

The unnaturalness of this singleness of will in respect of particular ends is reflected also in the emphasis Rousseau places on the collective identity of the individual, on the total alienation of the individual to the community, so that he becomes a communal person or citizen, and loses his natural identity as individual. It is true that Rousseau qualifies this claim by admitting the right of the individual to do what he pleases in what does not injure others (p. 131, note 2), and so to this extent Rousseau allows for the retention of the individual's natural identity. This individual freedom is acceptable to Rousseau since it directly reproduces the situation of the state of nature, in which each individual pursues his particular ends without regard for others. But where individuals in society impinge on each other, they cannot be allowed to retain their individuality and seek some relation among themselves which is the most satisfactory accommodation of each to the others. On the contrary a new collective identity must be created which can be substituted for the old. Thus Rousseau says:

In a word each man must be stripped of his own powers, and given powers which are external to him and which he cannot use without the help of others. The nearer men's natural powers are to extinction or annihilation and the stronger and more lasting their acquired powers, the stronger and more perfect is the social institution. So much so that if each citizen is nothing, can do nothing whatever except through co-operation with all the others and if the acquired power of the whole is equal to or greater than the sum of the natural powers of each of the individuals, then we can say that law-making has reached the highest point of perfection. (p. 52[1])

However, this citizen is a straw man. Having lost his natural capacity to move himself to his particular ends, he needs somebody to provide him with a motive principle. And this reflects the necessity, since only one particular end can be admitted, of somebody's end being represented as the common end and imposed on everybody else.

Rousseau's political theory consists in the running together of two very different accounts of the common interest as though they consti-tuted one coherent position. On the first account the common in-terest is the interest of each individual abstracted from its connexions with his actual particular ends and universalized. It is the interest of each in the liberty and security to pursue his particular ends what-ever these happen to be without being restricted by or dependent on others. This serves as a solution to Rousseau's social problem in so far as each recognizes the other only in respect of the other's abstract non-particularized existence. But it has an essential vacuity to the extent that it cannot take account of the actual particularity of men's ends. It consists precisely in attaining a common stand-point defined by its abstraction from the particularity of individuals and their ends. This vacuity is filled in by Rousseau by his transition to the second account of the common interest as a particular end. But a particular end as the common interest has to have the same character as the abstract common interest, namely it has to be the identical interest for each individual. It has to be true of this com-mon interest that the individual in pursuing his interest is necessarily pursuing the interest of all others, and in pursuing theirs is neces-sarily pursuing his own. Here each is related to the other not as an abstract or pure individual, but as an identical particular. Although the other exists for one as a particular, it is only as a complete dupli-cation of one's own particularity, so that one is again related to the

[1] I have found it necessary to depart from Cranston's translation in this passage.

other only as to oneself. However, the fraudulence of any such supposed identity is obvious.

Both accounts of the common interest are, however, solutions to the same problem. The essential political consequence of these solutions is the denial of any validity to social life, to social interdependencies of individuals and groups, apart from what is derived from the will of the community. Apart from the community's will only the individual and his individual existence for himself alone can be permitted. On the one hand we have each individual absolutely for himself, on his own, and on the other hand we have the all-embracing common life. For this is the condition that must be met if individuals are not to be dependent on each other in respect of their differentiated particularity. The essential requirement is to keep individuals in their particularity apart from each other, and so to break up all forms of group life which springs from the combinations and mutual accommodations of particular individuals in pursuit of their particular ends, and not from the united and single will of the common ego. Individual dependence on others is acceptable only if the others can be seen as servants of the common will. They do not then need to be recognized as particular individuals, but only as organs of the one super-individual, the collective person all equally constitute.

5

REVIEW AND CONCLUSION

Rousseau's intellectual effort in educational, moral and political theory is conceived as a solution to the problem that arises when natural men become aware of each other and begin to impinge on and conflict with each other. The natural principle is for each to pursue his own ends and to see others either as means or obstructions to them. The other in nature has no status except as means. He is not distinguished from natural forces. Each individual exists for himself alone. But in society others must cease to be treated as means, and must be recognized as having valid claims on one. The possibility then exists of treating the other in his particularity as an end for one, and so of aiming to please him as well as oneself and accommodate one's own particular ends to the particular ends of the other. The result is the mutual dependence of men in their particularity. The benign oneness of nature, the fact that each individual need take account of only one person, one will, one system of ends – himself and his own – is destroyed and replaced by a multiplicity of persons, wills and ends, each seeking accommodation with the others.

For Rousseau this is the worst possible social condition. It is an existence of corruption, of endless competition for superiority, and of depravity. The only hope for men lies in the reconstruction of society on the principle of nature, in the recovery of the oneness of nature. Each must come to recognize the other as an end for him, but must do so without recognizing him as a particular individual differentiated from himself. He must always be able to treat the other as a mere duplication of himself, so that in acting for the other, he is not acting for a different individual with different ends, whom he wishes to please, but only for the exact replica of himself and his own ends. The solution involves systematically conceiving of the individual's relations to others as relations to himself. It requires within the social framework the systematic abolition of the other.

It will be claimed that in so far as Rousseau's solution involves the recognition of the other as equally an end for himself, and so as having an equal right with oneself to pursue his particularity, the independent existence of others is being acknowledged and valued, and that it is precisely this attitude to the other that is absolutely necessary in order to value him as an individual. But the recognition and value he has for one is as an abstract, not as a particular, individual. His particularity has no value for one and must not have value. One is related to others as abstractions in order to be estranged from them as particulars. The whole point of the theory is the real estrangement from others that is made possible by an apparent moral recognition of and relation to them. But this is only achieved by abstracting the moral element from the real interests and real relations of men and by making it stand in opposition to them, so that it comes to deny and repress what it is meant to harmonize.

The absurdity and incoherence of Rousseau's theory lies precisely in the elaboration of a social ideal founded on a rejection of the right of individuals to live and value each other in their particularity. Since this is the source and content of the mutual affection which alone can, without tyranny, hold both small and larger groups of men together through all their conflicts, the denial of all validity to it, and its characterization as corrupt, is absurd, and can only ensure its replacement, as the essential social principle, by the despotic imposition of some people's particularity on others.

INDEX

Cambridge Studies in the History and Theory of Politics

TEXTS

STUDIES

IDEALISM, POLITICS AND HISTORY: SOURCES OF HEGELIAN THOUGHT, by *George Armstrong Kelly*

THE IMPACT OF LABOUR, 1920–1924. THE BEGINNING OF MODERN BRITISH POLITICS, by *Maurice Cowling*

ALIENATION: MARX'S CONCEPTION OF MAN IN CAPITALIST SOCIETY, by *Bertell Ollman*

HEGEL'S THEORY OF THE MODERN STATE, by *Shlomo Avineri*

THE POLITICS OF REFORM 1884, by *Andrew Jones*

FRANCOGALLIA by *François Hotman*. Latin text by *Ralph E. Giesey*: translated by *J. H. M. Salmon*

JEAN BODIN AND THE RISE OF ABSOLUTIST THEORY, by *Julian H. Franklin*